How Would You Like to Pay?

How Would You Like to Pay?

How Technology Is Changing the Future of Money

Bill Maurer

Duke University Press   Durham and London 2015

© 2015 Bill Maurer · All rights reserved · Printed in the United States of America on acid-free paper ∞ · Book and cover design by Natalie F. Smith · Typeset in Quadraat Pro by Tseng Information Systems, Inc. · Library of Congress Cataloging-in-Publication Data · Maurer, Bill, 1968– · How would you like to pay? : how technology is changing the future of money / Bill Maurer. · pages cm · Includes bibliographical references and index. · ISBN 978-0-8223-5956-2 (hardcover : alk. paper) · ISBN 978-0-8223-5999-9 (pbk. : alk. paper) · ISBN 978-0-8223-7517-3 (e-book) · 1. Electronic funds transfers. 2. Money. · I. Title. · HG1710.M38 2015 · 332.1′78—dc23 · 2015004994 · Duke University Press gratefully acknowledges the support of the Institute for Money, Technology and Financial Inclusion, which provided funds toward the publication of this book.

Contents

Acknowledgments

This little book took a long time to complete. First, because the world of payment was changing so rapidly during my writing. Second, because there are so many pictures I could have used to tell the story, and I am bad at making choices. Third, because I have taken the advice of friends and colleagues and tried to write this book in as accessible a format as possible. This is a challenge when you've written things like *Mutual Life, Limited: Islamic Banking, Alternative Currencies, Lateral Reason*—hardly examples of deathless prose. Many friends and colleagues provided photographs and ideas; those whose images I have used are acknowledged in the photo credits. I would also like to thank the entire community of researchers brought together by the Institute for Money, Technology and Financial Inclusion (IMTFI), as well as those who have helped sustain IMTFI over the past six years: Jenny Fan, John Seaman, Smoki Musaraj, Ivan Small,

Taylor Nelms, Elizabeth Reddy, Stephen Rea, Nick Seaver, Sean Mallin, Nathan Coben, Nathan Dobson, Jeff Katcherian, Sylvia Martin, Morgan Romine, Jake Kendall, and the Bill and Melinda Gates Foundation. Melissa Cliver early on provided some design concepts for a book such as this, and I thank her for the inspiration. Lana Swartz and Scott Mainwaring, along with Taylor Nelms, have been fellow adventurers in the payments industry. Two anonymous reviewers (who were subsequently revealed as Keith Hart and Bernardo Bátiz-Lazo) generously provided feedback and encouragement. I thank Peter Wissoker for acting as my agent and editor, and Ken Wissoker at Duke University Press for taking on this project and providing counsel throughout. The National Science Foundation (SES 0960423) supported research on payment technology. The opinions presented here are the author's own and do not reflect those of the National Science Foundation or any other organization. I would also like to thank Tom Boellstorff, Carter Wallar Ulaszewski, Gina Wallar, and Brian Ulaszewski for all of their love and companionship.

Introduction [Who This Book Is For]

This book aims to spur innovative thinking in anyone interested in the future of money.

Around 2007, I began research into the use of mobile phones as channels for financial services—the so-called mobile money phenomenon, primarily taking place in countries in the global South. Safaricom, Kenya's M-Pesa service, which permits people to send money to one another via their mobile phones, is by now legendary among those interested in the future of money, and it is what got me first interested in payment technologies. By 2014, however, services like M-Pesa occupied a newly exciting and crowded field. New startups in the global North with names like LevelUp and Boku harnessed smartphones for payment services; Apple launched a new iPhone payment system; and experiments like bitcoin, a digital cryptography based peer-to-peer payment system, started gaining traction—at least among venture capitalists and the tech world's media machine. A lot of people in the technology sector were suddenly thinking about money, its future, and how we pay for things—and how we might do so differently.

As I started talking and collaborating with professionals involved in creating new payment services, I was struck by the little revelations these professionals were having every day, the flashes of insight as they worked with and thought about money. Although I'd been writing and teaching about the cultural meanings and dynamics of money for almost twenty years, I was reminded just how surprising money can be once people start seeing it with new eyes. Mobile money and digital currency provocateurs and professionals were having the same kind of "ah ha!" moments that I had always tried to create for my students.

It is one thing to go about your daily life using money in various forms or via various technologies: coin, cash, check, plastic card, and now the mobile phone or other electronic devices. It is quite another to work at a firm or nonprofit where your boss suddenly tasks you with redesigning money and imagining its future. Many of the people I have interacted with and interviewed over the past several years have had the experience of abruptly finding money strange, unfamiliar, even improbable, and more open to change than they had ever imagined. In being jarred out of their commonsense assumptions about money, they had had a very anthropological experience: they had abruptly come up against the arbitrariness of a cornerstone of their world.

I.1 Using M-Pesa in Maasai country, Kenya (photo by Ndunge Kiiti).

In my conversations with such professionals I found that they appreciated the anthropological perspective on money's uses and meanings that I brought to the table, as well as anthropology's rich record of diverse forms of money around the world and throughout history. It offered a way to look more closely at their own money worlds, and the forms of currency and kinds of monetary practices going on all around them.

Given their generosity in allowing me into their lives and workplaces, I felt it time to return the favor, so I wrote this book with this diverse group of people in mind. They are computer programmers, artists, and interaction/user interface designers interested in money or working for payment industry startups; development practitioners looking at mobile money as a means of poverty alleviation around the world; innovative banking, finance, and telecommunications professionals charged with developing mobile or digital money systems and applications; silicon chip and device manufacturers wondering what always-online devices and embedded chips might mean for money; and advocates, activists, policymakers, bureaucrats, regulators, and others who seek to understand and to help shape the new technologies of money.

As we look back on the development of successful mobile phone–based money services like M-Pesa, or speculate about a future of digital currencies like bitcoin, we should not assume that they are the culmination of thousands of years of human cultural evolution, the next step in an ever-advancing trajectory. To do so would be to overlook the persistence of millennia-old traditions and institutions. Those traditions and institutions matter. Each new form for money co-exists and interacts with those that preceded it. Technology changes a lot, but not everything, and not all of the technology changes, either. Just look at the coins rattling around somewhere in your purse, briefcase, car, or sofa cushions — this is a technology that dates back nearly three thousand years, one that has remained remarkably stable in form and use. More interesting than trying to specify the direction of change, from my point of view, is to explore the interaction of different registers of meaning and practice when seemingly incompatible systems mix, and reach into one another and outward to new worlds.

This book seeks to open the door to those worlds so that people currently thinking about money might start thinking about it in new ways.

Many of the examples are taken from my own research and the research of others, including some of my undergraduate students at the University of California, Irvine. The latter have been collecting and documenting nonstandard uses of money in a course on the anthropology of money that I regularly teach. As a result, a fair number of the examples herein are from southern California. Others come from researchers supported by the Institute for Money, Technology and Financial Inclusion, which I direct. IMTFI has provided small grants to researchers around the world to explore people's existing practices involving money and other means of exchange and value storage. The purpose of the Institute is to gain a better understanding of what people are doing now, the everyday uses and meanings of money and other currencies, at a time when mobile telecommunications and digital technologies are transforming the everyday act of payment, and may be changing money itself.

I.2 Coins in automobile cupholder—an ancient but sometimes forgotten technology (unless otherwise credited, photos by the author).

In the course of my research, I have repeatedly been told it is still "early days" in the development of mobile money and digital currency. In fact, digital currency experiments go back many years. The original card networks that eventually became today's Visa and MasterCard began in the 1950s. Magnetic stripe payment cards go back to the early 1970s. In 1982, the computer scientist David Chaum devised a cryptographic protocol for untraceable, secure digital cash. He commercialized the idea and founded the short-lived DigiCash in 1990. PayPal, which permitted easy, secure person-to-person online money transfers, came into being in 2000. The combination of credit and debit cards, the Internet, and personal and later mobile computing changed how many people around the world spend their money and altered the experience of payment into an increasingly digital affair.

But not everywhere, not always, and not for everyone. Many lack access to bank accounts, either because bank branches do not exist in their community, will not accept low-value deposits, require identity documents people simply don't have, or actively or passively dissuade poor clients from stepping foot inside. Many lack access to the Internet. By 2012, 80 percent of the world's population had access to a mobile phone, mobile service, and electricity to charge the phone, even if they did not own the phone or subscribe to a service. It was only in 2013 that smartphones overtook basic feature phones in worldwide sales. While Apple Pay got a lot of media attention in late 2014, the simple feature phone is the star player in the story of how technology has changed the act of payment.

Mobile money services like M-Pesa are the first new digital

I.3 A clay money box for storing money, Nigeria.

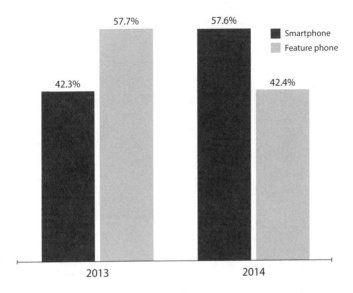

57.7% 57.6%

42.3% 42.4%

■ Smartphone
■ Feature phone

2013   2014

I.4 Feature phones vs. smartphones. Global worldwide sales of smartphones vs. feature phones ("Gartner Says Annual Smartphone Sales Surpassed Sales of Feature Phones for the First Time in 2013," Gartner Inc., Egham, UK, February 13, 2014, press release).

money platforms to have achieved any significant scale since the electronic charge card networks were created. In the short space of seven years since its launch in 2007, M-Pesa has attracted more than seventeen million customers, in a country of forty-four million people. By 2010, more people subscribed to M-Pesa in Kenya than had a bank account. Hence, development practitioners' hope that services like M-Pesa can become a route to financial stability and inclusion for people without access to or, more important, the means to afford a bank account.

I.5 Mobile money tackles global issues: Hope and hype in San Francisco, 2010.

Much initial excitement in mobile money focused on using the mobile phone as a means of facilitating the large-scale remittance flows that immigrants working in the developed world send to their relatives in their countries of origin. However, the success of early entrants M-Pesa in Kenya and GCASH and Smart Money in the Philippines, together with regulatory and technological hurdles around international money transfers, led many in the industry to focus on domestic, urban-to-rural money transfers.

M-Pesa is still the only mobile service that has really taken off, but its competitors are closing in, and other services are being rolled out in other countries. M-Pesa also changed the lives of the poor. But mobile money is at a crossroads. Will it really be a route to financial inclusion? Will it be a gold rush for businesses eager to make a profit from a new, untapped market segment, a bubble that will burst as soon as they reach the limit of fees they can glean from this new market, or as soon as they stop focusing on this market segment and seek out wealthier and potentially more remunerative customers?

M-Pesa also inspired many of the new "disruptors" in the global North, who seek to create new ways to pay for things, and even new moneys. So far, such innovations promise greater convenience, money-saving coupons, or special offers for loyal customers. Wouldn't it be nice if they could promise more? To begin to imagine what that "more" might be, however, we have to delve more deeply into money itself, and how it is that how we would like to pay can encode a host of alternatives for how we shall like to live.

1. Disruptions in Money

On August 8, 2012, there was big news in the world of payment. Starbucks, the coffee chain that brought double decaf lattes and mocha Frappuccino to almost every street corner in every big city in America, announced that it would begin processing all credit and debit card transactions using Square. It also announced a $25 million investment in the company. Square, Inc., launched in 2010, was the brainchild of Jack Dorsey, the web application developer who arguably changed the course of history with Twitter. This microblogging service proved its mettle beyond announcing the most banal of affairs ("coffee@#grncafe xtra good today!"), when people used it to help locate disaster victims after the 2011 Fukushima earthquake in Japan and to facilitate mass mobilization in the uprisings in the Arab world and the Occupy Wall Street movement later that same year. Twitter was a sensation: allowing users to send messages only 140 characters in length, from virtually any computing or mobile device, it is the kind of technology that is so simple you wonder why no one ever thought of it before. Square, Dorsey's second child, so to speak, is similarly genius: a small plastic square contains a magnetic stripe reader that detects and transmits the data stored on credit and debit cards through the earphone jack of a smartphone. Presto! Your phone has become a card reader; you have become a merchant capable of accepting credit and debit card payments. The technology is small, and the action it requires is familiar. It relies on a behavior—swiping a card—to which almost all consumers in the developed world have become accustomed. It does not require any new infrastructure save the tiny plastic square you plug into your earphone jack. Like Twitter, the technology takes a back seat to the functionality it affords.

Existing behavior. Existing infrastructure. Backgrounded technology. These three key elements can be found in another mobile phone-enabled payment system, but one that hit the scene several years before Square and that reached a scale so dramatic that even Dorsey would be impressed. This is M-Pesa, a service launched in 2007 that permits users to send money to others via a text message on their basic feature phone. The year 2007 is ancient history in the world of application development: consider the fact that the first iPhone was also released in that same year. M-Pesa revolutionized money transfers in Kenya, the site of its initial launch, and sparked enormous interest among development agencies and philanthropic organizations in the potential of the mobile phone to contribute to people's lives by providing them basic, safe, and affordable financial services.

1.1 Square at a Los Angeles coffee shop (photo by Alexandra Lippman).

Table 1.1 Formal or Informal?

Formal Economy	Informal Economy
generally regulated	generally unregulated
written contracts	unwritten agreements
regular temporal commitment for labor	irregular temporal commitment for labor
money transfers are reported to third parties	money transfers are not reported to third parties
lots and lots of records	sometimes no records, sometimes just as many as formal
generally taxed	generally not taxed
included in GDP	usually not included in GDP
governed by formal, legal rules and procedures	governed by social norms

Note: As Keith Hart has written, "informality is in the eye of the beholder. The informal economy does not exist in any empirical sense: it is a way of contrasting some phenomena with what we imagine constitutes the orthodox core of our economy" (http://thememorybank.co.uk/papers/informal-economy/).

In countries where bank branches are few and far between, and where they are only within reach of the relatively well-off anyway, having your phone serve as your access point for basic financial services like savings and money transfer can change your life. Indeed, in Kenya, by 2011, M-Pesa was in use by more than 50 percent of all households, and had processed in that year more transactions within Kenya than Western Union had done *globally*.

Like Square, M-Pesa harnessed existing technology and behavior: in this case, the text-message capability of all phones, and the everyday activity of sending a text message. It is simple. The technology is in the background. But the results have been profound. What is at stake is not just technological change or convenience, but bringing the poor and marginalized into the formal financial sector—for good or ill. The global financial crisis that began in 2008 may have given the lie to the goal of incorporating people into the formal sector. And banks have a terrible track record with the poor. At the same time, the alternatives to formal banks may not be much better and may expose people to increased risk of theft and high fees for informal money transfer or lending services. Certainly for the poor in Kenya, M-Pesa filled a need, solved a problem, and was widely adopted.

For its part, the payments industry—both the legacy players like the card networks and banks and the new "disruptors"—have long tried to convince people that cash is bad. Whether they tout its filthiness (and it is pretty dirty) or tell stories about its general disreputability (who walks around with a suitcase full of hundred-dollar bills? who really uses the 500 euro note?), they have a business interest in getting people to switch from cash to plastic or other electronic means of payment. Of course, their business models are based on transaction fees or, increasingly, transactional data for marketing purposes. Cash may come with costs, especially for the poor. Cash is cumbersome to transport and count, especially for businesses that take in a lot of it. But cash has a characteristic that other means of payment do not: it settles at par. That is, when I pay you a dollar for something, you get a dollar; not 99.8 cents (20 basis points or .2 percent off the top, the current rate for Visa debit transactions in Europe). One dollar, no more, no less. Cash is a state-based system, and it is publically mandated to settle at par. We pay a price for non-cash transactions. How should such a price be set? By whom? And who bears the cost? If we want to imagine a nonstate system, say, bitcoin, then what? Who ensures it works properly, and consistently? What happens when something goes wrong?

What is at stake is a matrix of questions: along one axis, whether new technologically enabled systems create second-class banking or even second-class moneys, whether cashlessness promises real benefits or merely another way to bilk people or profit from their digital personal data. Along another axis, whether the state has a role in money and payment, and what that proper role shall be. These are big questions, political questions, at the heart of the infrastructures of money.

Hype and Hope

In 2012, Square introduced its Square Wallet application for smartphones. No plastic square needed, one saves one's credit or debit card information with the application. When you are at a store that accepts this means of payment, you simply appear at the register and provide the clerk with your name. The clerk hits a button and you've paid. No extra device; no fumbling with your phone; nothing, payment is as simple as showing up. As with the Square card reader, Square Wallet was promising for three key reasons. It backgrounded the technological innovation, so the technology would not interfere with its use. It leveraged existing functions within the phone—in this case, the geolocation services that help you find stores near you that will accept the service, and that would allow the clerk's terminal to recognize that you (or, rather, your mobile device) when you enter the store. Finally, it did not demand any new behavior from its user. After all, you probably say your name a few times every day ("—Hi, it's Bill!").

It was a colossal flop. Unless you live in a tech hotspot like Silicon Valley, you probably never even saw it. The company pulled the plug on it in 2014. Square is not alone. There have been a number of new payment services launched since the release of the first iPhone. They are barely a ripple in a payments landscape still overwhelmingly dominated by cash and cards, debit or credit. And a number of them have had phenomenally bad luck. Exactly one week after Square and Starbucks announced their partnership, there was another news release. Major American retailers unveiled a new joint venture, the Merchant Customer Exchange, or MCX. Made up of Walmart, Target, Sunoco, CVS Pharmacy, 7-Eleven, Sears, and other name-brand retailers, MCX declared its intention to develop its own platform for processing payments via smartphone among its network of merchants. In 2014, on the heels of the launch of Apple Pay, MCX's payment application, called CurrenC, was hacked. Meanwhile, a consortium of the major U.S. carriers (AT&T, T-Mobile, and Verizon, together with American Express), formed ISIS, a mobile payment service piloted in 2011. It renamed itself Softcard in 2014 to avoid any association with the Islamic militant organization calling itself the Islamic State. Probably few consumers even knew of its existence until the media bump it received from its rebranding. Google launched GoogleWallet in 2011, in its gambit into the world of mobile payment services. MasterCard started a new PayPass product, allowing customers to use their phone at point-of-sale terminals enabled with its existing PayPass technology that had already been embedded into some of its cards. Citi, a partner in several of these mobile payment schemes, partnered with Jumio, a service that ingeniously turns the camera of a smartphone into a digital card reader—hold your card up to the smartphone camera and, without storing an image of the card, the camera detects and transmits the data needed to process the transaction. LevelUp, a similar service, creates graphic codes on the smartphone screen that can be read by another phone to transmit payment data. The iPhone 6 came equipped with Apple's own foray into mobile payments, Apple Pay. It's too early to tell how Apple's fingerprint-enabled payment tool will fare—but a few short weeks after it debuted, a number of major merchants flipped the switch on their point-of-sale terminals to disable its acceptance.

Despite the setbacks, however, the temperature has been steadily rising in the world of money, technology, and payment. In October, 2012, representatives from the diverse collection of companies and sectors trying to revolutionize how we pay gathered in Las Vegas for an event dubbed "Money2020," showcasing the latest in payments technologies and business models for processing transactions. Meanwhile, the online cryptocurrency, bitcoin, exploded on the scene when its value crossed the $100 mark in April, 2013. It nearly reached an exchange rate of $1,000 per bitcoin in November, 2013. By June, 2014, it stood at more than $600 and then fell to $350 by October. Despite the fluctuations, its impact on the imagination of application and service developers and their venture capital patrons could be seen at the next two "Money2020" conferences, where entire sessions were devoted to it (while at the conference in 2013, live demos of ISIS hit glitches during the plenary session, perhaps the most awkward time possible). Bitcoin proponents and representatives from bitcoin-related startups were starting to fall into two camps: those who stressed its role as a new form of money, and those who, more soberly, promoted it as a new payment protocol.

You would think that with all the large-scale players assembled here—the card networks like Visa and MasterCard, the mobile carriers like AT&T, companies like Google, device manufacturers like Apple, major retailers like Walmart—at least one of these new ways to pay would have taken off the way M-Pesa did in Kenya. Maybe the market has not been ready; maybe these are solutions looking for problems to solve; maybe no one has yet discovered the secret sauce that will lead millions of consumers in the global North to switch to mobile payments.

The turn of the new year in 2014 witnessed other developments—or, rather, disasters—in the world of money and payment. The giant retailer Target and the upscale clothing chain

1.2 Pay with bitcoin! Los Angeles, 2014 (photo by Alexandra Lippman).

Nieman Marcus were both targeted by hackers. In the former case, they stole more than forty million credit and debit card numbers; in the latter, they captured data from more than sixty thousand transactions. Then, in April, news broke that the SSL encryption protocol used by many online merchants had been vulnerable to attacks. People worldwide were advised to change all their passwords. In June, the Chinese restaurant chain P.F. Chang's also reported a credit card data breach and instructed its staff to process card purchases manually, using the old imprinting machines that probably few of its customers under age thirty had ever seen before. Data has been on people's minds, too, perhaps leading some to be skeptical of services that base themselves on the monetization of our "personal" data, from WikiLeaks to the U.S. National Security Administration, and just general consumer exhaustion with "targeted marketing," electronic means of payment whose business models are based on leveraging transactional data have yet to prove themselves in terms of profit or consumer adoption, acceptance, and trust.

Although its demise is frequently foretold, cash is still king—or, if it is not, it's like the old sovereign who steps in to save the day after everything else has failed. But why have these new systems not taken off like M-Pesa in Kenya has? Why, at the same time, are so many people and businesses so preoccupied with trying to find the secret ingredient that will revolutionize how we pay for things?

Money as a Means of Payment

To answer these questions, we need to understand *money*, and not how money has been conventionally understood, as a means of exchange. We are taught that money solves the problem of barter. When one party to a transaction has something to trade but it is not what the other party to the transaction wants, we have what the economists call the problem of the "double co-incidence of wants." Money, as a neutral medium of exchange that can be accepted for the purchase of any good or service, solves that problem. I may not have an item you want, but I can give you money to get what I need from you. My contention is that when we treat money solely as a means of exchange like this we depersonalize it, abstract it from all social relations save the most rudimentary, formulaic—and ultimately fictional—pure market relation. When we see money as a means of *payment*, however, we spotlight its technologies, how it moves from person to person or from Point A to Point B. We are confronted with its infrastructures.

The distinction between exchange and payment is a subtle one. Payment brings in all the other relationships, infrastructures, behaviors, and meanings involved in money. It also lets us think about instances where money is used in nonmarket ways, or in unreciprocated transactions. It lets us ask, how do we understand the basic practice of transferring value from one person to another? And how are new technologies like mobile and wearable computing, the so-called Internet of Things, and new distributed systems like bitcoin changing this most ancient of questions—*how would you like to pay?* Furthermore, how *should* we like to pay? What are the moral and philosophical aspects of payment that the collision of new technologies and money brings to the fore?

We have lived through a relatively brief historical period

1.3 Private banknote from the "wildcat" era, Bank of DeSoto, Nebraska, 1863.

of only 150 or so years when money was monopolized by the state. That is, governments issued currencies in order to facilitate exchange among their people and between their people and others in more distant lands. Prior to the invention of state-issued currency, a variety of private moneys circulated—as recently as the 1860s in the United States, there were around eight thousand currencies, issued by banks, railroad companies, retail stores, and other entities. The National Bank Act of 1863 began a decades-long process of consolidating the national currency in the United States, completed by the Federal Reserve system in the early twentieth century. The history of national money in the United Kingdom goes back further—but really, in the grand scheme of things, not by much. The Bank of England was founded in 1694 but pounds floated against gold and silver until World War I and precious metals could serve as a non-state money well into the twentieth century. Gold still occupies a place in the everyday monetary imagination: not coincidentally, "gold ATMs" or teller machines that look like cash dispensing machines started springing up around the world after the global financial crisis. For many people around the world, especially in places with unstable currencies and long traditions of using it as a store of value, gold has never lost its luster.

We may be entering a period again where private moneys come to the fore. Bitcoin has opened the possibility of a money maintained in a peer network without any central issuing authority or guarantor. Mobile payment services in the developed world allow you to receive digital coupons and rewards for your loyalty. Softcard (formerly ISIS) offered $10 Amazon.com gift cards for users who got their friends to enroll. Now, if points and coupons themselves become tradable and exchangeable for other vendors' products or rewards—if I can start to use my Starbucks Stars or reward points to get a discount at Walmart over the MCX system, for example, or if I can use an Amazon .com gift card on Apple's iTunes store—then has a new private currency been created, or a new private exchange that permits some but not all gifted funds to be convertible? Practitioners refer to open and closed systems: do payment systems permit exchanges across their own boundaries or circuits? What are the broader implications when they do not—for money, for society, for our in-built notions of access or equality? These and other questions occupy both developers of these new systems and regulators, as well as a few academics and political observers of the changing world of payments.

Payments are a complicated space. The business case for payment is counterintuitive, making money not by selling things but by providing the channel through which money passes—

Table 1.2 Bitcoin versus Mobile Money

	Mobile Money	Bitcoin
Unit of account	"e-money"	bitcoin
What that unit consists of	electronic coupon representing state currency	rights to transact in those units
Value of unit of account	backed by and equivalent to state currency	fluctuates according to demand
Issued by	licensed nonbank service provider	community of participants in the system
Payment infrastructure	mobile telecommunications network	blockchain database over Internet

Source: See Consultative Group to Assist the Poor, "Bitcoin versus Electronic Money," January 23, 2014, available at http://www.cgap.org/publications/bitcoin -vs-electronic-money.

building the "rails" over which payments are carried as a kind of freight. The field is crowded — by new startups like LevelUp, Zapp, Wave, and YellowPepper (some of which come and go quickly) as well as legacy players like Visa, MasterCard, wire services like Western Union, or, in the United States, the largely invisible Automated Clearing House (ACH), which sits underneath many credit, debit, check, direct deposit, and direct bill pay transactions, handling trillions of dollars in transactions each quarter.

What first got me interested in payments, however, was M-Pesa. This simple yet revolutionary service transformed the lives of millions of Kenyans, especially those in poverty. Led by philanthropic organizations like the Bill and Melinda Gates Foundation and government-aid agencies like USAID, the development community seized on so-called mobile money services as a means of poverty alleviation. If people did not have physical access to a bank, or enough money for a bank to bother with them, perhaps mobile money offered an alternative that could help people store their earnings and transfer money to others without the risk of theft or huge fees.

Along the way, those involved in fostering mobile money for financial inclusion discovered this complicated world of payments. And people getting into the business of payments discovered M-Pesa. Money itself had been a neutral, unnoticed phenomenon. With these rapid technological developments, money was foregrounded, open for debate and potentially for reinvention. The space has exploded not because people worldwide are flocking to new payment services or digital currencies — because they were not, outside of Kenya — but because such services captured the imagination of venture capitalists, programmers, designers, philanthropists, and probably the readers of this book.

But for me, the origin of the hype in M-Pesa and other mobile money services remind us of the link between payments and poverty. This link brings out the moral, political, and philosophical questions embedded in money. What is money? Should money be a monopoly of the state? Should there be competition in the means of exchange itself, not just the means of value transfer? When we focus on the payment side of money, and start inquiring into its infrastructures and the relationships it creates, what responsibilities and obligations attend the creation of new moneys and new ways to pay?

The rest of this book proceeds as follows. The next chapter starts with the question, what is money? It begins to outline a series of answers, emphasizing money as a technology, and the community or ecosystem, if you will, of other technologies and human relationships that surround money. One of those other technologies is the mobile phone, and the chapter briefly introduces the mobile phone. Chapter 3 introduces two imaginary characters—composites of real-life individuals—to illustrate the complex money and payment worlds of people along the spectrum of wealth and poverty. Chapter 4 retells the story of the evolution of money, moving the needle from exchange to payment and exploring along the way the relationships and practices that make money about much more than its value in exchange. Chapter 5 then dives into how people actually use money for all manner of things besides buying and selling things. The point is to understand the unexpected uses of this universal technology. We will see that money is always a moral technology, that people use it to make arguments, stake claims, acquire grace, and have fun. Chapter 6 takes you inside my own wallet and from there outward into a plethora of state and non-state currencies and people's everyday conversions between them. Chapter 7 then brings in the mobile phone, particularly the unexpected uses of this second-most ubiquitous technology after money. Understanding what people do with their phones can help us think about what they do when their money and their phones become increasingly linked to each other. Chapter 8 explores an early, unintended use of basic feature phones in the developing world that gave rise to mobile money services: the use and transfer of airtime credits. And chapter 9 comes back to the moral and political questions that money poses, every time we answer the simple question, "How would you like to pay?"

2. What Is Money?

What is money? The answer is changing as electronic and mobile communications devices become a new interface for storing, spending, paying, and keeping track of money, and as some in the tech world imagine an era of digital, nonstate currencies.

Many people involved in economic development are pinning their hopes for economic growth on adaptations of these new noncash systems, particularly with mobile phones. Others imagine libertarian utopias free from governments and insulated from inflation and economic shocks thanks to peer-to-peer cryptocurrencies. But can a new mode of payment or even a new currency bring about such substantial changes? To answer this question, we need to re-ask our earlier one: What is money?

Already in the wealthy Northern global countries money is taking many forms. Most people can be confident that, if they don't have cash in their wallet, they will usually be able to settle

Table 2.1 Mesopotamian Contracts and the Bitcoin Blockchain

Mesopotamia	Bitcoin Blockchain
records kept in central store-houses	records kept in a decentralized peer network
cuneiform tablet = records of one or a series of transactions	blockchain = entire ledger for all bitcoin transactions
clay "envelope" duplicates data on tablet inside	blockchain downloaded onto each participant's computer

Bitcoin, a digital currency experiment, avoids the "double spending" problem intrinsic to most digital moneys—how do you know the rights to a certain amount of value you've been given is not a duplicate of someone else's that has already been spent? This is not just a problem for digital moneys, but to any form of currency not tied to a physical token, to any form of exchange based on records rather than coins or bills. Bitcoin achieves this by maintaining a public record of all transactions in a database—the *blockchain*—that is distributed among the participants in the system. If everyone has a copy of the ledger, everyone can track what rights to value have been exchanged, although the identities of the transacting parties are quasi-anonymous. The massive replication of the blockchain means that no central authority has to maintain it and verify it. Instead, it is continuously verified by all the transacting parties. Records of transactions in the ancient Near East were sometimes similarly copied, as a way to prevent fraud and mitigate risks in a system where money was often a unit of account rather than a physical thing. The record on a clay tablet would be duplicated on an "envelope" that would completely encase the tablet. If there was a dispute about what was written on the envelope, transactors could break open the envelope and compare it to the tablet inside.

a bill for a purchase with a debit or credit card with a magnetic stripe or an embedded chip, a check, or, in some places, a plastic fob containing a contactless chip that deducts funds from their accounts. In such cashless transactions, is our money really with us? Yes, and no. Money can be any number of places when it is not with us.

Where Is Money?

Most of the people reading this book have a bank account—in fact, some may have several. Some people may even give account access to a family member or a friend in need. Many people also have some kind of credit accessible from a credit card issuer through cards enabled with magnetic stripes or chips embedded within them. Most also have a debit card, which pulls funds directly from their bank accounts. Such a plastic card can be used in a number of different ways. In addition to using it at a cashier's terminal to buy something—by having it swiped through a point-of-sale (POS) device, increasingly embedded directly into the cash register, or inserted into a hand-held device with a keypad for entering a PIN code—we can also enter the card number on a website and make a purchase, settle a bill, even pay a fine or a fee.

The infrastructure that allows for these transactions is hidden from us. So are the regulatory frameworks that ensure our money gets to where we want it to go, in the right amount, and within a reasonable period of time, without anyone else intercepting, delaying, or using it along the way. Often, the costs of using one method of payment over another are hidden from us, too. In many instances, the merchant bears them, and passes them on to consumers. We tend not to give it a second thought; however we choose to pay when we do so without cash, it just works, and we believe—usually—that it is secure. We also tend not to think about the nature of the value at the source of these transactions: that is to say, "our money," where it is, how it got there, and what it is doing while we are not using it.

Of course, we have a general understanding of how our money came to be: we earned it. We have a job—temporary, part-time, full-time, formal, or informal—and we got paid for our work. On the basis of that pay—its regularity, its magnitude—we may be extended credit, as well. It is so obvious that we do not bother spending much time worrying about the money in our accounts or the money we spend when we make a purchase using a card.

We rarely ever physically see that money, however. We may receive a check. For more and more of us, our paycheck is a digital transaction, a set of instructions from our employer's bank to our own instructing funds to be pushed into our account. We probably never see cash coming from our employer, or, in the case of direct deposit, that imaginary check, either. We see numbers on the screen or on a print-out. We see more numbers on a credit or debit card statement, which we read on the screen or, increasingly rarely, on a paper bill.

It all works. It works every time; or, almost every time. When it does not work, it either means something is wrong with our financial situation, or something is wrong with our employer, or something is wrong with the systems that support money and payment more generally. So, we tend more to worry about

2.1 Infrastructures of payment are hidden, except when they are not. Multiple point-of-sale terminals in the Rio de Janeiro Airport (photo by Jenny Fan).

getting or keeping that job, that source of money, and less time worrying about the mechanics of the money and its movements.

In many parts of the world, however, even in the world's wealthy countries, poor people do not have this choice in payment. Money means a cash economy. That is, how people pay is almost exclusively with physical tokens of state-issued currencies—paper banknotes and metal coins.

Cash gets the job done. But cash also brings problems. For one thing, its value can fluctuate wildly. It might be redenominated: overnight, the government issuing it can decide to change its value, remove some zeros so that one hundred becomes ten or one hundred thousand becomes one hundred. It can be lost or stolen, and, if it is, there is no way to track it.

It can also cost money to have money: to keep it stored safely, you need a minimum amount in order to keep a balance at the local bank, if there even is a local bank, or you may need to pay a person to store it for you. You may have to pay a fee to send money to another person far away from you, to pay for a service or a thing, to support your family, or to help someone out in times of need. You pay this fee to a money transfer agency. These can be formal, international businesses like Western Union, or informal networks of money transfer agents, and everything in-between. You may also have to pay some of your money to fulfill your religious duties, to demonstrate fealty toward your ancestors, and to prove yourself a worthy person in your community.

You might use several kinds of currencies at the same time, and this can also increase the cost of money, as you lose little amounts of it at each conversion between different forms of value.

2.2 Bundles of banknotes, Sierra Leone (photo by Ben Lyon).

You may live in a border region; you might frequently move from one country to another or buy things from people who are shuttling across borders; or you might live in a place where a foreign currency like the U.S. dollar is preferred over the local currency because it is more stable. In these contexts, you probably have to worry about counterfeits, and might refuse to accept certain denominations of paper money.

In addition to using state-issued currencies, you might use any of the following things as money, at least for some transactions: cattle, land, promises to use land, farm equipment, shells, and airtime minutes charged up in your mobile phone. You might store value in the form of gold or jewelry, or land, or cattle. You might get credit based on your social relationships with others, either cooperatively or through a patron to whom you owe social and monetary allegiance.

Your money world might be quite complex. The cash economy does not just mean "cash," and it certainly does not mean simple.

Phones and Money

More and more, this economy also includes the mobile phone. The number of mobile phone–based money services is rapidly increasing, especially in parts of the developing world where the mobile phone has become ubiquitous. In the wealthy Northern countries, there is less of a need for such services, because of the range and reliability of other payment systems. In many parts of the world, however, mobile money is filling a need. It is being added to the complex money world of cash economies and helping people transfer wealth more cheaply than the alternatives.

2.3 Goats as a store of value, Nigeria (photo by Isaac Oluwatayo).

It is also usually more secure than cash. It usually leaves a paper trail—well, an electronic trail—so it can be traced if lost or stolen or used from fraudulent purposes. It is also helping people to store wealth. From informal airtime-minute savings—purchasing airtime but not using it to talk, and cashing it out later (for a small commission, at a place that will do this often illicit or not-quite-sanctioned conversion)—to formalized systems for value storage with or without a bank account, people are using mobile phones as piggy banks.

Researchers studying people's use of mobile phones around the world have decisively established one key fact: phones are not just for talking. People have multiple and diverse uses for the mobile phone, and those use cases have to be taken into consideration in the design of new devices and services.

But researchers, policymakers, donors, and designers in the mobile money space are proceeding with one key—and flawed—assumption: that money is just used for its classically assigned functions, functions that have been taken for granted for hundreds, if not thousands, of years, but to which there is more than meets the eye: as a means of exchange, as a method of payment, as a store of value, and a measure of value, and as a unit of account.

In other words, people working on new technologies of money tend to assume that money is just money. But money is so much more, besides.

Money is also a system of relationships, a chain of promises, and a record of people's transactions with one another.

As the anthropologist Keith Hart has written, money is a "memory-bank."

Table 2.2 The Classic Definition of the Functions of Money

Money's a matter of functions four, a Medium, a Measure, a Standard, a Store.

—Alfred Milnes, *The Economic Foundations of Reconstruction*

Medium of exchange	used for buying and selling goods and services
Unit of account or measure of value	used to measure the value of all other things
Method of payment or standard of deferred payment	used to settle debts
Store of value	used to maintain and safeguard value that would otherwise diminish

Note: Although the method of payment function is often backgrounded in economics, alternative monetary theorists and many anthropologists foreground it together with the unit of account as central to its origins as a creature of the state to help govern the administration of the first large-scale, settled urban and agricultural societies.

Complex Money Ecologies

People in tech industries are used to talking about the different use cases for devices or applications: the ways people actually use their products or services once they are sent out into the wide world. Money also has multiple and diverse use cases. Or rather, moneys: the complex money ecologies of people around the world, and people's elaborate and diverse repertoires for using money as they navigate and add to those ecologies.

These ecologies and repertoires are not limited to the developing world, either. Once you start looking at money in terms of its actual use cases—what you really do with it in whatever form you use it—you start to see that our own money worlds are quite complex, too. That money is far more than simply economic. That our money is infused with meaning, morals, and material traces of our relationships with others. That money is about payment—relations, infrastructures, and meaning.

By providing examples of the use cases of money, I hope to spur the conversation about what money is, what it does, and what else it can do. The following pages and pictures are an open-ended prompt to think about using money, and to think about using it—and making it—differently.

3. Two Scenarios [A Day in the Money Life]

Clara lives in Boston. Every morning after she wakes up, she bathes, has breakfast, and walks across the street to the bus stop.

She takes a plastic card into which a radio-frequency ID (RFID) silicon chip is embedded. It contains data on the amount of value she has loaded onto the card. She taps the card on a card reader on the bus, and her fare is automatically deducted from the balance on the card.

When she gets off the bus at the subway station, she taps the card again in front of the turnstile in order to pass into the subway. It deducts the subway fare. When the card runs out of money, she can charge it up again at the metro station, using cash or her credit card. She actually gets a small discount for

3.1 Paying bus fare electronically, Cambridge, MA (photo by Stefan Helmreich).

using her card instead of a paper ticket: about twenty-five cents for each ride.

Clara would like to have her card charged up automatically, since she frequently forgets how much value she has on her card. She can do this by going online and registering for an automatic, monthly reloading service. She will have to provide a credit card number. She gets an added benefit for doing so, too: if she loses her transit card—and Clara frequently misplaces her card, and often worries that she has lost it—her unused balance on the card is protected. She can recover the value of her lost card by making a phone call to report that it has been lost. If the card is unregistered, however, and she loses it, that value is lost to her forever.

She gets to work, and begins her day at her computer.

On her breaks, she does some online shopping, using her credit card number. She gets reward points for using her credit card, and she pays off the balance every month to avoid interest charges and late fees. Sometimes, she also gets rewards or other offers for shopping with online vendors. There are some online vendors from whom she buys things quite frequently. Her credit card information is stored in their database, so she doesn't even have to enter it each time to make a purchase.

For her coffee break, she goes across the street to a coffee shop. She has a plastic gift card that someone gave her a few weeks ago and uses it to buy her coffee. In her purse, she keeps a whole stack of such gift cards from various stores, held together with a rubber band. On her way out of the coffee shop, a homeless man asks her for some change. Unfortunately for him, she

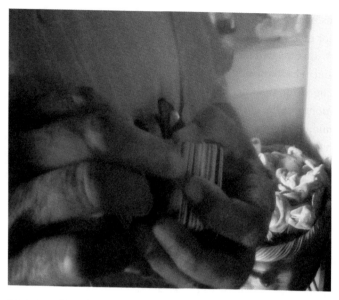

3.2 Lots and lots of gift cards!

doesn't have any: she rarely keeps coins in her pockets or purse. In fact, she rarely even receives them, since she hardly ever uses cash. When she does receive coins, often she puts them in a drawer in her desk and forgets about them. Right now, she probably has about three dollars' worth of pennies, nickels, dimes, and quarters sitting in her desk drawer.

At home, she puts her coins in a bowl on top of a bookshelf next to the front door. There are also some pennies on top of her washing machine.

Eventually, she tells herself every time she does laundry, she'll get around to putting them in a piggy bank or will try to remember to bring them with her to work so she can use them to buy her coffee.

But she rarely remembers.

At the end of the day, Clara shuts down her computer, gets back on the subway and the bus. She stops at the market before heading home, and buys some groceries using her debit card. She arrives home, puts her keys and her fare card in the bowl on the bookshelf next to the door. She did not receive any pay directly from her employer that day, but she knows that at the first of the month her paycheck will be automatically deposited into her bank account. She receives e-mail notification when this happens, but she hardly ever even opens the message because she is confident that the money will be there.

Meet Jany

Jany lives in Long Beach, California. When she gets up, she tries her best to get her three children to eat some cereal before they walk down to the bus stop to catch the bus for school. After they leave, she packs her husband's lunch and sends him off to his day job.

Her husband works for a landscaping firm that pays him every week in cash. He also does odd jobs in the evenings, also for cash. Jany manages the family's finances. She used to work in a dressmaker's shop before she had her last child. She sometimes takes in sewing work from her former boss or from her friends and neighbors, who pay her in cash.

She goes into her yard and collects some leaves from the lime tree on the small plot behind her house. She checks her basil plants and peppers. She uses these herself, for her own cooking,

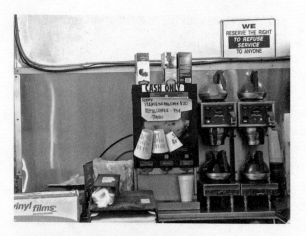

3.3 Cash only (photo by Alexandra Lippman).

3.4 Home provisions, Long Beach, CA.

3.5 Payment options and other services, Long Beach, CA.

3.6 Money trees in a Cambodian Buddhist temple, Seattle, WA
(photo by Thomas J. Douglas).

but she also shares them with some of her friends in the neighborhood, who, in return, often give her tomatoes, bananas, and sometimes papayas from their yards. When it is time for one of the several large festivals at the temple, she often gets together with her friends to make food for the monks.

She walks about a quarter mile to the nearest market. It is a small corner store, but it is packed with merchandise. There, she purchases some milk, eggs, and juice using a plastic card—much like Clara's transit card. This card is an Electronic Benefit Transfer (EBT) card, issued by the State of California as a means of providing her with monthly assistance. It has a magnetic strip on the back instead of an RFID chip inside of it. She swipes it through a special point-of-sale terminal—an EFT-POS—and enters her four-digit secret personal identification number (PIN). But she can only purchase certain items with it, and only uncooked food items. For the rest—soap, toothpaste, laundry detergent, and occasionally a roasted chicken or some fried fish—she unfolds a wad of cash she keeps clipped with a bobby pin in her dress pocket.

Later that day, she stops by the temple and makes a small offering of two quarters. She hopes to earn merit and also wants the monks to know she is a good woman who is caring for her family and her ancestors.

In her bedroom, she has a small wooden box under her bed in which she keeps the small amounts of cash she is able to save every week. She wants to send some money to her relatives in Cambodia in time for the new year. A friend of hers will be traveling to Cambodia, and Jany will give her these funds to carry with her—but not in cash. Instead, she plans to go to one of the jewelry merchants on the main street of her community and purchase some gold earrings and bracelets for her friend to carry to Cambodia for her. Her relatives in Cambodia sometimes still use special measurements for gold: damleung (1.02 ounces) and chi (0.13 ounces). Some of the older ones even measure the value of land in terms of damleung and small electronics in terms of chi of gold. Even though she was only a little girl at the time, she remembers when, from 1975 to 1980, the Khmer Rouge officially abolished state-issued money. So, like her older relatives, she still thinks gold is her safest bet, and she trusts her friend to make sure that the jewelry gets to its destination.

4. The Evolution of Money

Some of the fascination with mobile money or new technologies for recording and transferring value like bitcoin comes from the idea that they represent the next stage in this evolution of money, or, indeed, its pinnacle.

Advertisements for mobile phone–based payment systems sometimes exploit this. PayPal's iPhone application, which allows users to send small amounts of money to each other seemingly by simply tapping their phones together, was released with an advertising campaign that explicitly drew upon this evolutionary story. The ad included mock cave drawings, hieroglyphics, and even a narrator speaking in tones familiar to many people as those of a natural history documentary. The narrator identified the two human characters in the ad as "specimens," again invoking the familiar terms of popular natural history.

Similarly, the mobile phone provider Zain advertised its mobile money service, Zain Zap, with images of "ancient" systems of barter and money, before bringing the story up to the present or near future with the advent of its mobile service.

The evolutionary narratives are important not just because they have a starring role in advertisements. They are also important because they structure people's understandings of what money was, is, and thus what money—and mobile money—can become. And if we think money really did go through this evolutionary process, from barter, to shells, to coins, paper, plastic, and electrons, we risk making several related assumptions.

In the Beginning . . .

There is a common story about what money is, which is based on a common story about how money came to be. In the beginning, people lived in small communities of blood relatives and fended for themselves. They hunted and gathered for their subsistence, and learned how to weed out undesirable plants so that they would have easy access to plants that produce food.

As people became more adept at cultivation, populations grew. And people found that they could not always grow or procure from nature the things they needed in order to survive.

Trade was born.

People in different communities had surpluses of different goods. They traded these goods with one another. They established value and conducted their trade by bartering a certain quantity of one good for a quantity of a different good.

As everyone who has heard the story knows, the problem that quickly beset our primordial trader was that, more often than not, he could not find someone willing to accept his goods in return for what he needed. This is the problem of the "double coincidence of wants." In addition, his needs grew beyond the things his neighbors produced. And lugging around his own goods in sufficient quantities to trade became burdensome and impractical. Furthermore, stockpiling his surplus may have worked up to a point, but once the mice and the weather got at it, it quickly became worthless.

What to do? Invent money!

Here is where the story diverges, however.

In some accounts, the story goes that people decided to use a thing of value to them, and intrinsically recognizable as valuable to others, as money. It would initially serve as a means of exchange, and gradually would take on other of the classic functions of money as people expanded their use of it to include the payment of fines, tribute, or fees (as in ancient administrative states, tribute-based empires, or the tax collectors of the New Testament). Certain kinds of shells were good: they were pretty, of uniform size and shape, easily transportable, and durable. Precious metals were even better: they were universally valued; they did not rot, rust, or degrade; and they were easy to store and easy to transport.

In other accounts, the idea that certain things are of intrinsic value is considered implausible. The Enlightenment political philosopher, John Locke, while noting the virtues of precious metals for serving as money, also recognized that the selection of gold and silver as money was the product not of their intrinsic worth but rather of human convention. Herein lies an important

4.1 (*left*) A counterfeit cowrie: made of ivory, originally from the collection of Charles Opitz, a dealer in "odd and curious" money. Such objects were prevalent in Zhou Dynasty China.

4.2 (*right*) The Ghanaian 1 cauri coin, representing the cowries used throughout West Africa and the wider world.

4.3 Detail of a 5 kina banknote (Papua New Guinea), showing representations of shell valuables.

problem in the history of money: is it a commodity in itself, or a token of an existing agreement, an agreement in turn resting on a prior social relationship?

How one settles this divergence in the historical just-so story of money colors the rest of the tale. In one version, from using shells or precious metals or other objects desired for their durability, rarity, and beauty, people began to use tokens representing those metals. Shells, coins, marks on clay or paper, paper notes, plastic cards, electronic data proceed one after the other in a story of the gradual abstraction of money from its origin in, and foundation upon, universally valued commodities. Only with the end of the gold standard does money cease to represent real value.

Untethered from real value, money became something able to be manipulated by political interests and was thus corrupted, never again to be true. Hence, the periodic call from some political quarters for the past 150 years for the restoration of the gold standard and of supposedly real money.

In the other version of the story, however, money was only ever a representation of a relationship. The evolution of money, once it had been invented, is more properly understood as the shift over time in the use of different tally marks or tokens to represent that relationship. The objects mustered in procession in this history of money are the same as in the other version of history: shells, coins, paper, plastic, electronic data. Less frequently remembered are the clay tablets containing transaction records in cuneiform, the ancient accounting books of Mesopotamia, or the tally sticks with notches recording exchanges and payments in medieval Europe.

These evolution stories may lead us to some faulty assumptions. First, we might assume that each new form of money has replaced the last. Yet all we have to do is look in our own wallets and purses to see that multiple "stages" of money coexist in our own monetary ecology. We have coins, paper, and plastic. Plastic did not replace paper. Many of us also barter. And many of us mark certain kinds of monetary transactions with specific forms of money.

Second, we might assume that each new form of money is more efficient than those that preceded it. More efficient means better, means more progress. For economists, it means cheaper. But are new forms of money really more efficient? They often come at a price, after all. What does efficiency mean? Efficient for what purposes, and when? Credit cards are extremely convenient, fast, and easy to use, until you are stuck in a place that only accepts cash, or the taxi driver's point-of-sale terminal is broken and he forgot to bring along the old carbon-copy credit card forms. For merchants, there is a cost to the efficiency of credit cards, too, in the interchange and other fees the merchant has to pay on every card-based transaction.

Efficiency can mean speed. But there are many times when we want to slow down transactions: to have a cooling-off period before we make a hasty purchasing decision; to savor the act of gift giving and gift receiving. From giving silver dollars to reward a child, to sending a check in a card or converting credit or cash into a gift card for use at a particular store, we frequently use other forms of money to mark the special quality of a gift

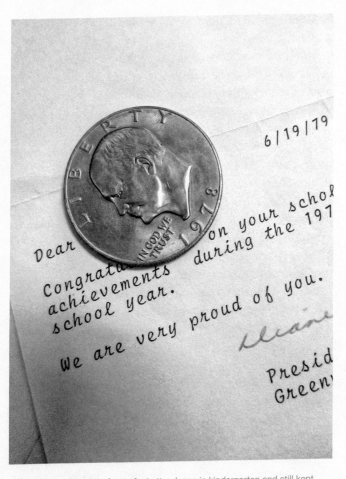

4.4 A silver dollar, given for perfect attendance in kindergarten and still kept out of circulation.

by making gifted money less convertible, less liquid, and less efficient.

Third, and most important, if we buy the evolution story, we might lose sight of the infrastructures that support each new form of money, not to mention the infrastructures that allow the different forms to be converted into one another.

We might start thinking, for example, that currencies in on-line virtual worlds like World of Warcraft have been created out of thin air. We are tapping into an important insight in this thought, but we're not getting it quite right. It is not that money can come into being sui generis, by "fiat," as the phrase goes. Rather, it comes into being by convention, agreement, and a set of relationships and obligations among people inside of complex organizations like states.

Because we are not accustomed to seeing these conventions or relationships the way we see objects like paper bills or images on the screen, we overlook them. It is not that money is "just" a relationship. It is that all that we are, as social beings, is "just" relationships." These relationships include our moneys.

These relationships also include all of the technological, legal, and regulatory, organizational and communicative apparatuses that make money, and that make it work, in its various forms. An often-used joke in end-of-the-world movies has the surviving characters playing Monopoly or poker with "real" U.S. dollars. The joke is that, after the destruction of governments and infrastructures that breathed value into dollars, paper currencies are revealed for how worthless they always really were.

But they were not worthless originally. They may have been paper; but those pieces of paper indexed a vast and powerful apparatus for creating, assigning, managing, and distributing the collective wealth.

Infrastructures of Value

Some of those apparatus, or infrastructures, are more visible than others. We don't easily see the regulatory frameworks that ensure that our money will be accepted by a merchant, that our payment card will be charged the proper amount and without any hidden fees at the point-of-sale, that we have redress in case of a bank error.

We do see some of the technological infrastructures in the form factors of our payment systems: coins and paper, plastic cards with magnetic strips, RFID or NFC chips that enable tap-and-go services. In the global North, mobile money systems generally take advantage of RFID or NFC chips. Transit systems already use them, people are familiar with the tap-and-go concept, and embedding or overlaying a chip onto a mobile phone is relatively easy. There is a great deal of excitement in industry quarters about NFC-enabled smartphones. The card breaches of 2013–14 led many in the industry to predict big changes in how people pay for things in the United States. Chip-and-pin cards, like those used in Europe, will soon become the new standard.

In the developing world, mobile money services rely on some of the technological infrastructure of the mobile phone and the mobile network that are not immediately apparent to people in the developed world. Many rely on programs written on the SIM card inside the phone. Short-message service (SMS) is familiar because of text messaging, but can be harnessed for money services, as well.

4.5 The M-Pesa SIM card.

Unstructured supplementary service data (USSD) is a protocol like SMS that can be used on almost all mobile phones regardless of manufacturer or network operator, and it, too, is being harnessed for mobile money services. It requires the user to initiate a session with a special code. Once the session is established, the users phone remains connected in a secure channel to the server until the user logs out.

SIM, SMS, and USSD services can run on low-end phones, which are still the great majority of phones on the planet. Sales of smartphones exceeded feature phones globally for the first time in 2013. But feature phones for mobile money have some important benefits. SMS and USSD mobile money applications have the potential to be both device- and carrier-independent. This means that you could send money from any phone on any mobile service to any other phone on any other service—if the service is set up that way. Some mobile operators, seeking to build their customer base through mobile money, have resisted doing so.

How easy would it be to create a new form of money, by fiat, just like the state has done? Some of the people working to develop new forms of electronic and mobile money dream of "disintermediating" banks and creating privatized, nonstate currencies. The reality at the moment, though, is that most electronic and mobile money systems depend on a prior existing bank account, whether the client's own or the mobile money service's.

Local and Alternative Money

That doesn't mean it's impossible. Alternative and complementary currency proponents have succeeded, on a small scale, in

Table 4.1 SMS and USSD

SMS	USSD
Short-message service	unstructured supplementary service data
Normal text message sent from user to user	the data sent between a phone and a mobile network operator to indicate the phone's location and for functions like balance inquiries
One-way transmission	two-way transmission
Store and forward: the phone sends a message to the mobile network's server that holds the message for routing to Its final destination	real time: the phone and the server open a channel that remains open while messages are transmitted back and forth
Relatively standardized between mobile network operators	no set standard between mobile network operators

4.6 The Ithaca HOUR, a local, complementary currency.

creating local moneys that circulate in small, geographically bounded regions, alongside state currencies. Yet even these financial innovators have found that there is more to creating money than just running a printing press or a chip shop.

So, while the evolutionary story of money makes for good marketing, allowing service providers to make the case that they are offering the latest evolutionary stage in money, the picture is more complex.

Look again at our characters in chapter 3. They are both using multiple forms of currency at the same time. This includes barter, which still exists, even in the developed world. The peer-to-peer economy represented by platforms from Craigslist to Airbnb, though not without controversy, seems to be leveraging the same kinds of relationship and networks as barter or complementary currency experiments like Local Exchange and Trading Systems (LETS)—albeit with a centralized, corporate ledger garnering huge infusions of venture capital for their founders.

The evolution story usually benefits certain players—particularly those who want to dominate the money landscape, and perhaps even wrest it from the control of the banks, to say nothing of the banking regulators. Money for these people is just another consumer good, and the industry players who use the evolutionary story want to dominate the market for this good.

Money is a special good, however. It can't work without the technological and regulatory infrastructures enabling it. The evolutionary story leaves out the regulatory and consumer protection architectures that are necessary to make any new money and payment systems function. The state will enforce the payment of a debt in its money—but you are largely on your own if you want help enforcing a debt in your own private token or, at least, having it treated as a real debt. The state will also usually only accept its own money for the payment of public debts: taxes, fees, tolls, and fines. Here we see clearly money in its means of payment aspect, indicating the state's power to create money, trumping its means of exchange aspect, and the market's power to set prices.

The evolution story also leaves out the fact that people do all sorts of things with money besides earn it, pay with it, and save it, let alone that people are already doing all sorts of things with the "latest" stage in the evolution of money—the mobile phone.

First, however, let's look more closely at what people already do with their money.

5. Use Cases for Money

Although people rarely see the interpersonal relationships and regulatory infrastructures underlying their money, there are countless ways in which people every day make social relationships visible using money.

The early twentieth-century philosopher Georg Simmel both celebrated and feared the ability of modern money to allow an anonymous society. Complete strangers could use money to buy and sell. Their obligations to others ended as soon as the transaction was completed. Simmel saw this as good insofar as it freed people from old feudal bonds or relationships of patronage or political favor. Those were the kinds of relationships that required that a person buy from or sell to only a small set of individuals or else risk sanction or punishment.

Whether feudal tribute or protection money, we like to think that these kind of monetary relationships have been left behind in the past. We declare optimistically that our freedom today is defined in part by the fact that we can use our money anywhere, to buy and sell with anyone.

Aside from the fact that tribute, slavery, and extortion are sadly alive and well today, there are countless other ways in which people try to direct the flow of money to create, reflect, or maintain specific ties.

In doing so, whether they realize it or not, they are momentarily challenging the anonymity of money and interrupting its universal fungibility, its ability to be exchanged for anything. This chapter presents only a small sample of what I will call "use cases" for state-issued currency. Just as the mobile phone is more than a communication device for talking, state-issued money is more than what you'd think.

When software engineers and systems analysts employ the term "use case," they are referring to the possible scenarios in which a program they are developing might have to respond to input coming from the outside — from an unpredictable human, for example. Anticipating use cases can theoretically help the engineer or programmer design a better, more useful system.

It also means accepting the fact that people do all kinds of unintended things with the systems and devices they encounter.

We all develop workarounds, "just-so" practices that help us navigate the technological and other systems in our lives, ways of getting things done sometimes in spite of the best laid plans of those who created the systems. Mobile phone researchers have documented rich and varied use cases for mobile communications devices around the world. These will be discussed in chapter 7.

It is important to understand money's use cases—and the use cases for monetary alternatives—in order to get a clearer understanding of what money is, and how people do things with the diverse currencies they encounter in their daily lives. Imagining future scenarios for money and payment, like those envisioned for mobile phone–based or novel online moneys or payment systems, requires a deep understanding not just of the mobile phone or virtual environments, but of money's use cases, too.

Gifts and Rituals

Let's begin with a straightforward use for money: as gifts.

People make gifts of money all the time. When they do so, they often enclose it in a wrapper or mark it somehow to indicate that it is special. The tradition of enclosing cash or a check in a card is not just to shield the contents of the envelope from prying eyes or potential thieves. It is also an important point of etiquette. Enclosing the money seals it away from the sphere of the market or commercialization—at least momentarily—and places it into another realm.

The rituals that accompany the use and, importantly, the thanks reciprocated for the money gift similarly strive to maintain its sanctity or separateness from the market. One does not use gifted money on sinful purchases. But one is not supposed to use gifted money for mundane purchases, like paying the electricity bill, either. Any book of etiquette will tell you that one does not thank the giver by directly acknowledging the denomination of the gift or even its monetary nature. Instead, one thanks the giver "for the generous gift" with which one purchased "a new bicycle" or "a new shirt." The wrapper in effect

5.1 A gift for Chinese New Year.

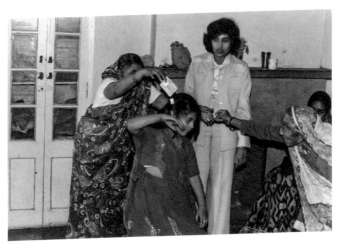
5.2 A wedding dollar dance, 1970s (photo by Parul Aggarwal).

remains around the money gift, even after it is removed and the money spent.

Money gifts mark important temporal cycles, such as the stages in the human life course and special times of the year. People make gifts of money to one another at the birth of a child, at baptism, at marriage, and at funerals. The dead often take money gifts with them into the grave, the laying of coins on the eyes of the dead or the placement of a coin in the mouth being a once-widespread custom that persists in some cultures to this day.

At baptisms, engagements, and weddings, coins or paper currency may be simply given in cards or other special wrappers, or may be thrown at, rubbed on, attached to, or flamboyantly waved over the recipients. People give cash to recognize a

5.3 After the wedding (photo by Maya Manolovits).

graduate's successful completion of schooling, either in cards or in elaborate garlands or leis.

The bills from a lei are supposed to be put toward the expenses of starting out on one's new life. Often, however, the funds are used to thank the giver: by taking the giver to a fancy dinner at a restaurant, for example, or, if the amount is large enough, taking the giver on a vacation.

Gifts of money mark ritual cycles as well, such as people who celebrate the Chinese New Year by placing money in special envelopes as gifts. People celebrating the Persian New Year in the United States take two-dollar bills and mark them with special inscriptions before giving them to each other. In some parts of the United States, these specially marked banknotes turn up in change around that time of year. From dropping a coin in a box

5.4 A money lei, Huntington Beach, CA.

before lighting a candle in a Catholic church, to crafting elaborate money trees in a Cambodian Buddhist temple, or leaving money at the crossroads in the Caribbean or the far east of Russia, people use cash and coins as religious offerings in a wide variety of traditions and rituals.

In some cases, the money is imagined to stand in for a sacrifice of food, incense, or an animal. In other cases, money's magic—its embodiment of value despite its mere existence as a mundane, physical object—is associated with the magic of the divinities.

In still other cases, the gods, because ineffable, are imagined to consume money's ineffability, just as many deities are imagined to consume the smoke from a burnt offering.

Significantly, in many countries, money offered to religious institutions is afforded special treatment in the tax code. In a sense, its holiness persists, and it continues to give back, even after it has left the pocketbook of the giver.

People use legal tender in any number of rituals related to luck. People toss coins into public and private fountains—even great works of art that incorporate fountains! Wishing wells sometimes incorporate elements of games of chance, too. After all, what does one wish for in throwing a coin into a well but to receive more coins? In some parts of the world, people write messages or prayers on paper money in the hopes that that bill will return to them a thousandfold.

Some money rituals are also related to luck and protection during travels. The Imam Zamin is one such practice. A coin or bill is placed in a special pocket or scarf wrapped around the traveler's arm before a journey. At the conclusion of the voyage,

5.5 Obsolete Indian coins marked with red vermillion at Diwali, the Hindu festival of lights. Photo taken in Irvine, 2004. The vermillion is put on the coins during prayer, while the flowers are placed after prayer (photo by Parul Aggarwal).

5.6 and 5.7 Offerings of coins, Altai Repubic, Russia (photo by Svetlana Tyukhteneva).

5.8 A prayer for luck and money.

5.9 Imam Zamin, a tradition of wrapping money in a cloth around the arm to ensure safe travel, Irvine, CA (photo by Tasneem Siddiqui).

the traveler removes the scarf and either donates the money or uses it to purchase food to celebrate with friends his or her safe arrival. In the United States, some people carry two-dollar bills in their wallets for good luck. Around the world, people make knots out of bills—often U.S. dollars, no matter what country they live in—and hold them in their wallets.

Fun and Politics

Cash and coin serve as political tokens, too.

People write political messages on state currency, because it is literally a representation of state authority. Whether to pro-

5.10 A folded bill, carried for luck (photo by Julian Bleeker).

claim the economic might of a subordinated population, to condemn the state that issued the currency as illegitimate, or to layer onto the currency the dream of another, future state, people use the means of exchange as a means of political expression.

Money is also fun to play with.

Coins are satisfying to hold, flip, throw, spin, hide, and recover. Paper bills can be cunningly folded, ripped, burned, drawn upon, and modified in a host of ways. Money is one of the magician's favorite props. The act of destroying value by tearing up a bill or making a coin disappear always creates excitement in an audience, and the relief at seeing the value restored always draws applause. Magicians play on the mystery of paper and metal, worthless objects in themselves, signifying value. Banknotes can be folded like origami paper and the resulting paper given as gifts, kept as curiosities, or put at the bottom of a jar next to the cash register to encourage tips.

Of course, people also modify other currency objects to make them personal, to politicize them, or to add to them another brand—even to supplant the brand of the national currency itself.

Thus, people add decals to or punch holes in their credit cards. People design their own bank checks to include political messages, protesting war spending, for example. And merchants offer branded debit cards or gift cards, replacing the names of the banks with the name of the store. They also modify receipts, including a special message to customers to pique their interest and keep them coming back.

5.11 A political statement: an Indonesian banknote overstamped, "Islamic Republic of Indonesia."

When people modify state-issued currency, they add meaning to it. They slow down its circulation and limit its fungibility. They insert other values into market values. They express their hopes and their faiths, and they cement and sometimes sunder their social relationships with one another, with the country in which they live, and with the wider market and political communities of which they are a part.

6. What's in Your Wallet?

Promises, Obligations, and Debts

Empty your wallet, purse, pockets, money clip, or whatever you have on your person in which you carry your money.

What's inside?

Some readers of this book may have no cash at all, if they mainly use plastic cards. Others may have some cash and many cards of different kinds. But there are probably other things in your personal money carrier besides state-issued currency or technological devices like cards to help you access state-issued currency.

You may have receipts, which provide a record of your recent transactions, as well as your whereabouts over the past few days or weeks, and your tastes and everyday activities.

What else is in your wallet besides cash, cards, and receipts? You probably have proof of identity. In many parts of the world,

6.1 The contents of the author's wallet.

however, a simple means of verifying identity is hard for most people to acquire. It can be a vicious circle: living in a favela or slum or in a remote rural area or on the streets of a megacity, you have no proof of a fixed address, no record of having continuously paid electric bills or water bills, and probably no official record of your birth. That makes it difficult to get a state-issued identity card, and this, in turn, makes it nearly impossible to open a bank account. So, you pay more to save your money and to transfer it to others in times of need.

Many people carry with them a host of objects that serve some of the functions of money, at least some of the time or in certain locations. These objects are rarely convertible into one another, at least not without a lot of effort.

If you have a store-branded gift card or a paper gift certificate, you cannot convert it back into cash, and you can only use it at a specified location. Loyalty cards that provide extra savings at the supermarket or help you earn points toward discounts or money-saving coupons provide another kind of value that is also not fungible. Some new web-based businesses allow people to trade their loyalty points with one another, even to convert loyalty points to cash. But, when you are at a merchant's cash register and it is time to pay, and you have no cash or credit cards, it would be a tough sell to convince the merchant to accept your loyalty points at the supermarket or frequent flier miles from an airline, even if you had the ability to quickly and easily transfer them.

Many wonder whether such things are heralding a new form of privatized, nonstate currency. Several national and state jurisdictions have regulations around "noncash payment products"

6.2 A basic loyalty card of indeterminate value, Portfolio Café, Long Beach, CA.

like loyalty cards, coupons, and gift certificates. Consumer protection, antitrust, trade, and other regulations govern such noncash payment products.

There are simple, everyday examples, too: the coffee card that rewards the repeat customer with a free cup after the tenth or twelfth purchased. Hand-stamped loyalty programs have always fascinated me. Some have a fixed value—one small coffee after ten drinks of any size. Others have a more flexible, indeterminate value—any drink, of any size, after ten drinks. The difference in monetary value can be considerable. Hand-validated cards also add a human element to the transaction: a new employee might hesitate to stamp the card if the customer is buying a drink on the borderline of what would be considered the norm, say, a small juice as opposed to a cappuccino. And a longtime employee might be inclined to add additional stamps "for free" or redeem a completed card for more than one drink, or for a really expensive, special concoction.

So, things like loyalty cards and other noncash payment products are only partially fungible. They are also in some cases only partially pegged, in a direct and easily quantifiable relationship, to their equivalent in state currencies. They are examples of what sociologists and anthropologists have called "special purpose" or "earmarked moneys."

Transit cards and tokens are another example of special-purpose money. Interestingly, in some parts of the world, transit cards sometimes accumulate enhanced fungibility—and functionality—as money itself.

In Japan, contactless Suica cards were developed for use on the transit lines but came to be accepted as a form of payment

6.3 Using a Suica card in Japan, originally a transit card repurposed for general payment (photo by Scott Mainwaring).

by merchants at kiosks selling small goods in the train stations. What began as a special purpose, private currency pegged to the state currency has grown into a means of general-purpose payment, albeit still ultimately pegged to the state currency.

Money without the State

What about money not tied to state currency?

Cattle, land, forests, alcohol, tobacco, shells, fabric, and furs: all have, at one time or another, served some or all of the classic functions of money and most have been used to express promises, obligations, and debts. In many parts of the world, they still are.

6.4 A long-term investment: planting trees in south India (photo by Thanuja Mummidi).

Some communities print their own money. If others agree to accept it in exchange for goods and services, it can work. This is legal in the United States only if the money is not minted — it cannot be a coin, for historical reasons having to do with powers reserved in the Constitution for the federal government — and so long as it does not resemble the U.S. dollar. Income earned in a local or complementary currency must be reported on federal income tax forms, under the category "Barter."

And what about barter? While our ancestors may have exchanged eggs for corn, today you can barter computer services for auto repair. Likewise, a plumber may do repair work for a dentist in exchange for dental services. At least in the United States, the fair market value of the goods and services exchanged must be reported as income by both parties.

You Can Take It with You

Then there are the things that look like money but that do not work as money—for living humans, at least.

Many people around the world offer real money or representations of money to their dead ancestors or the deities. In some cases, they imagine that the dead or the gods require these currencies for their affairs in the afterlife or spirit realm. Chinese "hell money" or "ghost money" is a familiar example.

Spirits have been known to only accept certain denominations or currencies—the anthropologist Heonik Kwon reports on the "dollarization" of Vietnamese ghost money, the Vietnamese dead demanding joss paper in the form of U.S. dollars. People also offer the dead representations of credit cards, gold bars, even mobile phones and airline miles.

Although it may sound like a joke, ghost money is serious business. Its association with the dead lends it an eerie, uncanny quality, even for people who do not believe in it. In this, it participates in the uncanniness surrounding many of the objects used as tokens of value.

Ghost money and nonstate currencies raise an important point about money's forms, and the ecologies within which these forms commingle.

These forms always mark social, political, and economic status. This is obvious in the case of money for the dead—since they are, after all, dead, and thus a distinct social status or rank.

6.5 Chinese hell money.

It becomes less obvious, and more interesting, as we observe different people using the things in their wallets that sometimes do and sometimes do not work as part of their monetary repertoires, the everyday exchanges and conversions they make with state and nonstate money.

Prisoners use cigarettes and jet-setters use airline miles. While the latter have more options, the former are probably better at making quick conversions and exploiting small differences in value, the spread on the different currencies at their disposal.

7. What Can You Do with a Mobile Phone?

Researchers who study the widespread diffusion and rapid up-take of the mobile phone document the varied use cases for this new technology. In the process, they have discovered that the mobile phone is not just a communication tool. It is also not linked to one person, one phone number, or one service provider.

Almost as soon as mobile network operators built cell towers, and device manufacturers and carriers plied mobile phones around the world, people found new uses for them—they inserted them into their existing social relationships. They cracked them open (figuratively and literally).

They brought the phone and the mobile service into their existing material, spiritual, social, and technological practices in ways few in IT labs or corporate strategy divisions ever anticipated.

Many readers of this book are probably familiar with the way that mobile phones have been used to coordinate mass demonstrations and protests around the world, from the Philippines to Iran, Egypt, the United States, and throughout Europe. Text messages sent from person to person or blasted to a wide network of phone numbers can create large-scale rallies or document human rights abuses or voter intimidation and fraud. Videos and photographs help protesters document police or military abuses, and help get the word, and, crucially, images about a rebellion or revolution to the outside world.

Mobile technology also helps track disease outbreaks and monitor aid delivery. The basic functionality of most mobile phones allows information exchange that can generate and sustain social movements and development aid.

Many readers of this book may be able to use their mobile phones to check e-mail, view a web page, download a document file, play a multiple-player game, watch a movie, take a picture or a video, and deposit a check or make a payment. For the average human being, however, still in 2015, the mobile phone does not have a camera, let alone the computer-like functionality of high-end, application-heavy smartphones like the iPhone. Rather, most mobiles are low-end "feature phones" that can place and receive calls and send and receive text messages. The modal mobile may also have a small LED flashlight, and it might have the ability to allow the user to play a simple video game.

The technological limitations of more basic phones do not hinder people's creativity in using them, however.

A Shared, Flexible Resource

To understand how most people use most mobile phones, we need to lose some of our preconceptions about what the phone is, who owns it and its constituent parts, and how it can be used.

People in the global North tend to assume that the phone someone carries in his pocket belongs to him and him alone. We assume that he subscribes to a service that provides access to the mobile network he signed up for, as well as roaming access to other networks as needed, often for an additional charge. He receives a bill in the mail or online at regular, probably monthly, intervals. He keeps his phone with him pretty much all the time. He might even sleep with it next to his bed, turned on, using it as a flashlight in the middle of the night and as an alarm clock to help him wake up in the morning.

A quarter of the world's population lives in poverty. About 15 percent of Americans — more than forty-six million — live below the poverty line. Simply put, many people cannot afford a subscription to a mobile network service.

That does not prevent them from using a mobile phone, however.

Even the poor can purchase a phone without subscribing to a service, and, instead, buy airtime as needed, "topping up" their phone whenever they run out of minutes.

In the global South, people who cannot afford a phone can often purchase just the SIM card that goes inside a phone, which is linked to a service provider and contains their account and identity information. They then use someone else's phone, inserting their own SIM card into the phone to make a call or send a text message.

7.1 A man in Afghanistan with his four working mobile phones (photo by Jan Chipchase).

Conversely, people may own multiple phones and/or multiple SIM cards. Having a number of phones or SIMS allows them to take advantage of differences in rates depending on whom they wish to call, since calls to people on the same network are often cheaper than calls to people using other networks.

Having multiple SIMS also allows people to take advantage of differences in reception of different cell signals in remote regions or across national boundaries. Having different SIMS in some places now also means having access to different mobile money services. I might be an M-Pesa customer and a Zain Zap customer, switching out the SIM cards if I want to cash out at a particular location, or if I want to make transactions across carriers but minimize the fees I have to pay.

If we imagine mobile phones are held onto by one person,

and used by only that one person—then we miss the family dynamics and social relationships that support shared-phone use in the developing world. Understanding shared use may lead to an evolution in the design of new systems.

Some phones support multiple address books, and thus facilitate sharing. And phones can be hacked to allow dual or multiple SIMs.

Many Patterns of Sharing

There is a host of patterns of phone and SIM sharing. One example is step messaging. It may be that the recipient of a call or SMS is not the intended recipient of the message: instead, the person receiving the message understands that his role is to carry the message—on foot—to the person for whom it is intended.

Sharing phones and SIMs is not limited to the very poor, but extends through middle-class consumers, as well. The central point however, is to disentangle ownership from use and make no assumptions about the personal, private, or individual nature of the phone.

Likewise, other people often mediate the use of the mobile phone. If one does not possess the necessary technological, literacy, or numeracy skills to use the technology, usually there is someone nearby who does.

For people with little means of proving their identities, maintaining a digital identity over time can be truly significant. Mobile technology can facilitate this, and here the mobile comes to be not just a device for communication but also for creating and maintaining a verifiable identity.

7.2 At the airtime kiosk, getting assistance (photo by Ben Lyon).

Of course, when the purchase of mobile service or a SIM card requires identity documentation, the potential user of the mobile phone can get caught in a vicious circle. However, mediated use can step into the breach, if, in addition to providing shared service, the intermediary is willing to vouch for a person's identity.

Intermediaries are also crucial for aspects of mobile phone use that people with a smartphone in the developed world rarely ever think about: getting electrical current to charge the battery, getting the software necessary to run a device and to add more interesting or useful content like ringtones and wallpapers, and getting spare parts or fixing the phone when it needs repair.

One common use case for the mobile phone is the "missed

call." Known by different names in different places—beeping, fishing, pranking, flashing—although it may look the same to an outside observer, researchers have shown that there are differences in how and why it is done.

The practice involves placing a call to someone but disconnecting before they can pick up, allowing the recipient of the call to know that you called, and to collect your number in their recent calls list. But no one has been charged by the service provider for the call.

One Practice, Many Meanings

In effect, the missed call tells someone else, "I am here." But there are differences in what the missed call means depending on place, context, relationship, and regularity.

It can simply be a signal to communicate a prearranged message: "I am ready to be picked up," or "I am at the market now." It can also be a demand: "Call me back" or a demand with an additional moral injunction: "Call me back, you can afford it and I can't."

Businesses exploit the practice, too: "Send a missed call to 443–23–4553 to contact the owner." Friends and family use missed calls simply to affirm that they are doing okay, to obviate the need for a lengthy and expensive call.

While missed calls demonstrate careful financial management of the mobile phone, pointing to the strategies people have for preserving their precious airtime and using their minutes wisely, this is not the entire story. The key to the missed call is its context and its execution.

An outsider observer would see different instances of the

7.3 Using "missed calls," Bangalore, India (photo by Rikin Gandhi).

same thing: someone receives a call, but the caller hangs up before the recipient can pick up.

From the inside, however, the relationships involved, the social and economic context, even the style with which the missed call is made—disconnect after one ring, after two rings, after five rings; or two or more missed calls in rapid succession—marks the missed call as a different practice each time.

This is central: part of the art of the missed call is in how it is done. As the philosopher Gilbert Ryle noted, an involuntary twitch of the eyelid is different from a wink. And as the anthropologist Clifford Geertz carried further, a conspiratorial wink is different from a parody of such a wink, and so forth.

The observation should lead us to ask about the twitches and winks of the diverse use cases of the mobile phone. People ex-

7.4 Using mobile money, Sierra Leone (photo by Ben Lyon).

press themselves through mobile use, but not just with voice, text, and images sent over the phones. They express themselves with how they send voice, text, images, and things like missed calls, the manner or style with which they do so.

So, too, for money: throwing a coin in a busker's guitar case is different from tossing it; crumpling a bill and leaving it as a tip is different from folding it over once, diagonally; from placing it on the table; from placing it in the hand or, more firmly and deliberately, in the palm.

Tossing a bill or coin in a card game or dropping money reverently into a box at church; offering with spite or offering with pity; a quick beep of a missed call to say, I am alive!, or the repeated, insistent beeps of a multiple flasher demanding you call someone back and insinuating—without words, text, or images—that you are a greedy bastard if you don't. We are already seeing people express themselves with mobile money— using it to conceal transactions from spouses, or to advertise payments within a social group. The repertoires of mobile and money represent a web of use cases not always captured by our commonsense assumptions of what mobile and money are, are for, and can do.

One of the most remarkable of these unintended uses of the mobile phone may be the transformation of the phone into a money management tool, and the conversion of mobile airtime into money.

8. Airtime

You have a top-up phone. You prepay for the calls you want to make, with units of time denominated in terms of units of currency. When you need airtime, you go to a kiosk or a store and purchase a card.

The card is usually made of heavy-stock paper with a rectangular latex laminate covering a small portion of it. You scratch off the latex to reveal a code. You press a special sequence of keys on the phone, and, when instructed either by a voice or on the screen, you enter the code from the card.

You have successfully topped-up your phone, and now have more airtime with which to call or SMS your friends and family members.

Now imagine what might happen in the following scenario.

8.1 Buying airtime in Afghanistan (photo by Jan Chipchase).

You need to buy a schoolbook for your daughter. You live in a rural area, about forty miles away from the nearest bookshop.

Your friend, however, lives in town, close to the shop. You want her to purchase the book for you and give it to your daughter, who lives in a dormitory in the same town.

You purchase an airtime card from your local kiosk. Instead of entering the sequence of keys that allows you to top-up your phone, you send your friend a text message containing the code on the scratch card, along with your request that she purchase the book for you and give it to your daughter.

She now has a number of options. If she uses the same mobile network as you do, she can enter the code into her phone and top-up her own phone. She can then use the equivalent amount of cash, and go purchase the book for you. You've given her air-time in exchange for her giving your daughter a book.

Or, she can go to a kiosk that sells airtime. She might do this if she is not on the same network as you.

The vendor might be willing to buy the airtime code from her, in exchange for a small commission. He can then resell it, per-haps also on commission, either by reselling the code directly to another phone customer or by topping-up his own phone and charging others to use it to place calls.

In either case, the vendor will provide your friend with cash in exchange for the airtime code. And your friend can take the cash to the bookshop and purchase that book.

Airtime transfers happen informally all the time, all over the world. Many services now allow the consumer to send airtime directly to another phone.

But the use of airtime as money, and airtime transfer as value transfer, opens up the whole world of "mobile money": mobile phone-enabled money storage and transfer systems. Airtime transfer is another element in the cash economy. The fungibility of airtime with cash depends on the making of airtime into a unique commodity that can be bought and sold. We first need to be able to conceptualize minutes spent talking in terms of money.

Most billing plans for mobile service explain that a certain amount of money gives the consumer a certain number of min-utes of talking time on the phone. It gets more complicated, however, when text messages are added into the mix, which may be charged on a per-message basis, a per-bundle of messages

8.2 Loading airtime in Afghanistan (photo by Jan Chipchase).

basis, or a per-unit of time (week, month), not to exceed a maximum threshold. It also gets complicated with the added fees for using airtime to talk with someone on a different network.

Regardless, people using airtime to transfer value are quite sophisticated at calculating the discount rate of the practice—a combination of the various fees levied by the mobile operator, the cost of buying the top-up card itself (including the transportation costs to the closest airtime vendor), and the commissions taken by the middlemen. All told, in spite of these costs, sending value via airtime is often less expensive than sending value via an established wire service, to say nothing of a bank.

But airtime transfer raises a host of questions and some trenchant regulatory and security issues, as well.

For example, most banking regulations require that banks make an effort to confirm the identity of their clients. This mitigates the potential for banks to be used to launder money. If I can set up an account with a fictitious name and address, and then use funds for nefarious purposes, no one can trace those funds back to me. So, most countries have requirements for identity verification at the time of the opening of a bank account.

Such "Know Your Customer" (KYC) requirements are a key component in countering the financing of terrorist activities, as well. Most mobile service providers have less strict identity requirements. And usually, anyone can purchase an airtime top-up card, without having to produce any identification. On the other hand, however, it is precisely the high KYC requirements of banks that keep many of the poor away: if I don't have an identity card, birth certificate, or fixed or formal address, but need a safe place to store my money, I will not be welcome at most banks.

Some countries have adopted "proportionate" regulations in recognition of the difficulties KYC presents to the poor consumer. Proportionate KYC might include a maximum threshold on the amount of money a customer can transfer and specify the number of transactions that a customer can make in a given period of time. If the customer wants to do more, then ever-increasing degrees of verifiable identity documentation must be provided.

In addition, imagine what would happen if everyone with airtime decided they wanted to cash out at their local kiosk. The vendor would need to have enough cash on hand to make sure everyone received their money. But what if the vendor simply did not have enough cash one day? Like a run on the bank, a run on an airtime vendor could have far-reaching consequences for people's trust of the mobile carrier, the vendor, and other intermediaries. Banks have reserve requirements—a minimum amount of liquid assets on hand at all times—to mitigate the risks of any potential run on the banks. Most countries also provide deposit insurance up to a certain amount: if the bank should fail, your deposits are insured by the government and will be repaid in full up to that maximum threshold. Should telecommunications companies have the same? What if you top-up your phone and your phone company goes out of business?

Banks are also required to handle the assets that people store with them in certain ways. They can loan and invest them, but within various regulatory limits. And they must provide a rate of return for their use of those funds, too. What happens with the funds held by a mobile network operator whose customers are using airtime as a means of value transfer? Furthermore, suppose someone purchases airtime and, instead of using it to talk, or transferring it to someone else, just lets it sit there, almost like putting coins in a piggy bank or a deposit in a bank? What should the mobile operator do with the "float," the money held by the mobile operator in between the time of the purchase of airtime and its dispersal as talk or as value to another person?

Furthermore, at the level of monetary policy, should airtime float be considered a part of the money supply?

There are other, more mundane, matters as well. What if you add airtime to your phone and someone steals it? What if you lose your phone? If it were a credit card, consumer protection laws would provide you with some recourse. What if the airtime vendor starts charging exorbitant rates? How should he set his rates, in the first place? Airtime is also only fungible if a vendor is willing to convert it freely into cash. In most places, the conversion back into cash is informal, illicit, or even illegal. But if people are using airtime as money, should the vendor be required to back-convert airtime into cash?

It was not until mobile carriers launched mobile money services that regulators began to worry about these kinds of questions. As long as airtime minute transfer was happening informally, as part of the cash economy and the everyday monetary ecology of people around the world, it escaped the regulators' attention. Airtime transfer captivated the imagination of people in the telecommunications, banking, and microfinance industries, as well as design researchers and people studying the use of the mobile phone. As more and more mobile money services come into being, all of these regulatory issues, and more, are vexing the world's central bankers, monetary authorities, and consumer protection advocates. Several countries, notably Kenya, the Philippines, and South Africa, have been leading the way in adopting proportionate and carefully thought-out regulations for mobile phone–based money services. But knowing what people already do with money itself, the myriad use cases for currency objects around the world and the complicated ecologies and repertoires for money and mobiles, it is probably only a matter of time before someone does something that neither the designers of these systems nor the regulators have ever imagined. What happens after that is anyone's guess.

The point, for now, however, is the following: airtime transfer is one of those unexpected use cases of the mobile phone. It is also, at the same time, one of those unexpected use cases of money. It offers a clear example of why we need a better understanding of what people do with mobiles, and with moneys, in their day-to-day lives.

9. Monetary Repertoires

Even people in the global North, with relatively stable state currencies, bank accounts, and markets—the global financial crisis notwithstanding—operate with several different kinds of money, and do so with style, whether they realize it or not.

When we chose one form or payment over another; when we earmark money for special purposes; when we wrap currency objects in cards and in relationships; when we use other things to serve some of the functions of currency, we demonstrate the diverse use cases for money and our repertoire of practices for animating those use cases. We forge relationships and make moral or political statements. We also give lie to the common misperception that money is just one thing, and that one thing is just what mainstream economists say it is.

In this respect, there is nothing special about what mobile phones or mobile money services or even online, virtual currencies do to money. They simply add to what was already there: a complex ecology of payment that we use to make our relationships with one another—for good, for ill, or just for fun. But right now, mobiles and other digital currency experiments do make explicit that complex ecology, and call to attention different people's repertoires for managing that ecology. If we've never sent money by cellphone before, we learn something new about our own money world when we see someone effortlessly using SMS or USSD to transfer money to another person. If we try to use a virtual currency or bitcoin, we are confronted with a series of questions about our everyday, backgrounded money infrastructures. How do the funds get into my bank account when my paycheck is deposited? What third-party entities help facilitate a credit card transaction? Even though it looks instantaneous, when does my transaction actually settle? We start to ask questions about what money is, about how payment happens, who or what controls it, and about how it all came to be.

More Accessible Than a Bank Account

As discussed earlier, many observers of mobile money (and, truth be told, many promoters of mobile money from a business perspective) see it as the last stage of money's evolution. Many also see it as a silver bullet for poverty alleviation. Since the mobile phone is ubiquitous, available even to those who do not own one, and relatively cheap, it is more accessible to more people than a bank account.

Ever since its beginnings around 2000, in the minds of some experts and in the launching of some pilot projects, to its take-off in 2007 or 2008, with the widespread attention given to

9.1 A GCASH promotion: register for a mobile money account, and get a green metal cash box with a padlock (photo by Anatoly Jing Gusto).

M-Pesa in Kenya, and GCASH and Smart Money in the Philippines, mobile money has captured the imagination of people seeking to alleviate global poverty.

M-Pesa began as a microfinance loan repayment system. GCASH and Smart helped people send money to their relatives on remote islands. Mobile money has its origins in the goal of financial inclusion: bringing millions of people without access to bank accounts—the "unbanked"—into the formal financial sector.

This goal is based on a number of underlying assumptions. One of these is that getting people into formal financial systems is better than allowing them to continue to use informal systems.

Formal systems can seem detached, abstract, and untrustworthy. For many people, keeping cash under the mattress or gold buried under the floorboards makes more sense than opening a savings account, even if they have the means to do so. This is especially the case in countries where currency values fluctuate wildly, banks routinely fail, and governments are corrupt.

The sociologist Viviana Zelizer has documented the myriad ways that poor people's money in the nineteenth century was an object of intensive intervention on the part of various state, civic, and religious actors seeking to "uplift" the lower classes morally and spiritually, not just financially. Money was an integral part of social and religious programs for training, disciplining, and oftentimes controlling the poor in the name of modernity. Monetary practices of poor people were arguably also important in the very conceptualization of them as "the poor," a clearly identifiable group or class for whom other well-meaning agents then devised programs. To the exhortation that researchers and developers be attentive to the diversity of monetary repertoires, then, the following additional caution must be added: people working in this space must acknowledge their position in a long history of powerful others descending upon the poor and their money. This is especially important because of the prominent role of large-scale industry actors operating to provide services with the aim of profit.

We have to remember that state-issued money is a kind of public good. The private rails of the payment industry charge tolls on the passage of money. Adherents of bitcoin or other currency experiments may want to escape both the state and the centralized systems of for-profit payment service providers. If

9.2 Mobile money can pose challenges for the visually impaired
(photo by Ndunge Kiiti).

they do so, however, they also rescind their right to recourse if anything goes wrong. And they may end up creating new closed or gated systems, inaccessible to all but the wealthy, or able-bodied, or tech-savvy.

Choosing Payment, Currency, Community

"Monetary repertoire" is a concept I borrow from the anthropologist, Jane Guyer. It emphasizes the practical unfolding of people's actions involving money and currency objects. It allows for the element of performative mastery and style in the use and negotiation of diverse monetary ecologies and what Guyer calls the "horizons of contingency" within which people operate.

Sometimes poor people view saving state-issued currencies as the wrong solution—or even a contributor—to their problems. The very word "savings" produces discomfort because it underscores people's fear that they never have enough money on hand. It also evokes fears that powerful elites will use money in a gambit to acquire poor people's resources: land, livestock, or other illiquid wealth. We should never forget that poor people have good reason to be ambivalent about state-issued currency, banks, and savings accounts.

As one researcher insightfully remarked to me, "Money is more than just money." It can also index relationships of obligation, rank, clientage, social belonging, or state sanction. People calculate the amounts of such payments often outside of market exchange relationships: they are not set by market price but often arbitrarily, or ritually, or as the outcome of a formal or informal political process. Why does a parking ticket cost $47? Why is a good luck offering made in multiples of eight?

9.3 A bank line, Haiti (photo by Erin B. Taylor).

This brings me back to some of the questions about money and poverty with which I began this book. Much research to date on the poor and their money overlooks people's complex monetary repertoires. Existing research frameworks flatten the diverse monetary ecologies in which people generally operate, and the multiple systems of calculation, scales, and standards of value, temporal cycles, and forms of literacy and numeracy with which they do so. When researchers acknowledge, say, the use of cattle as a kind of currency, they still often treat all quasi-moneys as commensurable into one another: as all money or wealth, equally fungible, and able to become liquid under the right conditions.

This is hardly the case, however, even in Western industrialized societies. We still maintain what anthropologist Annette

9.4 Televangelists accept donations by M-Pesa in Kenya.

Weiner called "inalienable possessions" (heirlooms, keepsakes) and place moral boundaries around some pockets of our money (the child's piggy bank, the swear jar) or boundaries of convenience around others which, nevertheless, are rather difficult to dislodge (the change in the car's ashtray or in the desk drawer). Pennies are treated differently than quarters. Tapping into the child's piggy bank to buy groceries evokes pity. Doing so to buy drugs or alcohol elicits contempt.

Even modern, Western money, then, the supposedly flat wash into which all things can be dissolved, the rational and rationalizing force in contemporary commodity economies, is, on closer inspection, a complex delta of rivulets, side currents, eddies, and pools. It is also a record of relationships extending across space and in both directions in time, linking us to our ancestors, descendants, and fellow humans in a vast network, giving us — if we just look carefully — a picture of ourselves as a species in all our diversity and complexity.

And it is a value descriptor and standard of comparison in

conversations about worth that carry implicit ethical, political, or moral judgments.

Understanding money therefore means not just understanding legal tender. It means understanding quasi-currencies, alternative currencies, and a range of objects of wealth and value that sometimes serve some or all of money's classic functions, and that help us register credit and debt to one another—that help us forge connections. Again, for good or for ill! Dominance is one kind of connection, after all. Community is another. Community does not always mean harmony, just as dominance does not always mean hierarchy.

This is a decidedly different stance from the perspective that relegates physical assets (land, livestock, vehicles, capital equipment, jewelry, special ritual items) to the sidelines. Indeed, illiquid assets and the way that people convert objects into and out of legal tender may be extremely significant in some contexts. It may be quite rational for poor people to try to convert their money into land, cattle, or jewelry as quickly as possible, given currency instability, inflation, or corruption.

Might mobile money start to work like an illiquid asset in some contexts and for some people? When police officers in Afghanistan started to receive their pay via mobile phone, payday became a private affair. People could not make claims on their cash because the police officers were no longer seen to be leaving the place where they received their salaries. Since cash is so liquid and can be readily given hand to hand, people felt they could make claims on it. What about the mobile phone? On the one hand, it can facilitate easy and long-distance transfers of wealth. On the other hand, if the fact of payday can be kept

9.5 Gold and gift cards, Los Angeles (photo by Alexandra Lippman).

relatively quiet, then workers might have an easier time holding onto their pay. Mobile money might help people sequester value, much as livestock help people sequester value in many parts of the world today.

Planning the Future of Money for the Poor . . . and Everyone Else?

Too often, technologists, development planners, and government policymakers assume that money is something that people need to be helped to hold onto or to use more productively, however that may be defined. People may get more of it, but its roles in the social, cultural, religious, and technological machinery, so to speak, are ignored.

But what else is money for the poor—or for anyone, really? A prestige item? A spiritual force that taps into other such forces, like the power of numbers, abstractions, ancestors, gods, or high-status people?

When Stuart Rutherford's groundbreaking book, *The Poor and Their Money*, dispelled the myth prevalent in some policy circles that the poor were "too poor to save," the discourse—and practice—shifted. Recognizing that poor people already want to save and, in fact, have a number of ways to do so at their disposal freed up development and policy professionals to look differently at the poor and their money. The shift that took place can be characterized as a shift from pathology to epidemiology.

Before, some in the development and policy community saw the poor as constitutionally incapable of saving. Either they were simply too poor to save, and/or they lacked the foresight, discipline, or financial literacy skills to enable them to save. After the conceptual shift recognizing that the poor can, want to, and do save, however, practitioners became convinced that the poor, having already demonstrated a number of informal savings arrangements in their portfolio, simply needed assistance—treatment—in order to achieve their (and others') savings goals. The epidemiological discourse is not just an extended metaphor: the methodologies of choice in assessing design and adoption of new saving services by major players in this space is the randomized controlled trial (RCT), taken directly from clinical biomedical and epidemiological research. Trials come complete with control groups and treatment groups. And, indeed, RCT-based studies can be useful for understanding factors impacting uptake and adoption of new services.

To an anthropologist, however, it is striking how this shift in recent work on financial services for the poor replicates the old ethnographic problem of relativism. Are "the poor" radically different from "us," or are they just like us, only poorer?

Anthropology still struggles with the relativism/universalism issue. Many anthropologists, in attending to the processes and structures that continually make and remake social and cultural worlds, defer this question by asking how apparently irreconcilable difference is itself a product of various social forces and practices.

Anthropologists also question why Westerners perennially seem obsessed with the problem of difference while other peoples, not part of the history that attempted to create isomorphism among race, language, culture, and nation—may simply note it but move on. Following this lead, the issue could be framed differently: neither that the poor are different and

9.6 Collecting funds for a temple, Seattle, WA (photo by Thomas J. Douglas).

thus poor, nor that they are similar but only poorer and in need of assistance or treatment. Rather, they are stitched into modernity's institutions and processes in ways that work well in some cases and not so well in others (as we all are, really).

This uneven connection results in a Byzantine network of confounding practices, beliefs, trajectories, and social and technical arrangements. People send out grappling hooks of their own making into the institutions and processes of modernity, thus making it anew—and they actually make it what it is, in fact, since "modernity" itself is as much convenient fiction as description of a total or complete project.

This network can be visualized in the complex and unexpected infrastructures that poor people around the world cre-

9.7 The coconut water man, Santa Monica, CA—note the iPhone with a Square reader, to accept payments anywhere (photo by Alexandra Lippman).

ate for themselves all the time to gain access to utilities like water or electricity.

Just as technologies afford all kinds of uses for which they were never designed or intended, just as technologies can be hacked or tweaked or wired together with other technologies to create new assemblages that do different things, so too with money. The difference is that money is not just a technology. It is an extension of relationships, between ourselves and others, our pasts and futures, our world, and the worlds we can imagine.

So: how will we reimagine money?

For Further Reading

1. Disruptions in Money

On the possibility that we are entering a new era of private currencies, see Edward Castronova, *Wildcat Currency: How the Virtual Money Revolution Is Transforming the Economy* (New Haven, CT: Yale University Press, 2014).

On the origins of national, state-based currency as the global standard, see Eric Helleiner, *The Making of National Money: Territorial Currencies in Historical Perspective* (Ithaca, NY: Cornell University Press, 2002).

The best introduction to the payments industry in the United States is Carol Benson and Scott Loftesness, *Payments Systems in the U.S.: A Guide for the Payments Professional* (Menlo Park, CA: Glenbrook, 2010).

The GSM Association of mobile network operators maintains a comprehensive database of mobile money deployments around the world.

The Consultative Group to Assist the Poor (CGAP), a consortium of government-run aid agencies housed at the World Bank, produces working papers on mobile money for poverty alleviation.

Other helpful introductions to the world of mobile money include the following papers: Jan Chipchase, "Mobile Phone Practices and the Design of Mobile Money Services for Emerging Markets," http://www .janchipchase.org/fp/wp-content/uploads/presentations/JanChipchase _DesigningMobileMoneyServices_vFinal.pdf, Jan. 2009; Jonathan Donner and Camilo Andres Tellez, "Mobile Banking and Economic Development: Linking Adoption, Impact, and Use," *Asian Journal of Communication* 18(4): 318–332, 2008; Richard Duncombe and Richard Boateng, "Mobile Phones and Financial Services in Developing Countries: A Review of Concepts, Methods, Issues, Evidence and Future Research Directions," *Third World Quarterly* 30(7): 1237–1258, 2009; and Ignacio Mas and Olga Morawczynski, "Designing Mobile Money Services: Lessons from M-PESA," *Innovations: Technology, Governance, Globalization* 4(2): 77–91, 2009.

2. What Is Money?

The concept of the cash economy used here as well as the notion of repertoire is borrowed from the work of the anthropologist Jane Guyer, whose *Marginal Gains: Monetary Transactions in Atlantic Africa* (Chicago, IL: University of Chicago Press, 2004) is required reading.

The idea of a "money world" is borrowed from the work of Catherine Eagleton, formerly curator of paper money and modern coins at the British Museum's Department of Coins and Medals and author, with Jonathan Williams, of *Money: A History* (Richmond Hill, Ontario: Firefly Books, 2007).

Keith Hart's seminal text is *The Memory Bank: Money in an Unequal World* (London: Profile Books, 1999), and the commodity/token distinction comes from him.

Supriya Singh's *Globalization and Money: A Global South Perspective* (London: Rowman & Littlefield Publishers, 2013) speaks to many of the same concerns as this book.

For an introduction to bitcoin, see Chris Clark, *Bitcoin Internals: A Technical Guide to Bitcoin* (Amazon Digital Services, 2013).

Bill Bryson's *At Home: A Short History of Private Life* (New York: Doubleday, 2010) has a wonderful section on the domestication of the telephone.

Dave Birch's *Identity Is the New Money* (London: London Publishing House, 2014) offers fascinating insights into how emerging payments systems work in tandem with and sometimes in contradiction to big data and security.

3. Two Scenarios

An early treatment of the nonbank services used by the poor in the United States is John Caskey's *Fringe Banking: Check-Cashing Outlets, Pawnshops and the Poor* (New York: Russell Sage Press, 1996). Often, such alternative financial institutions are criticized for their lack of transparency around fees and interest rates. However, conventional banks have also been taken to task for their often inscrutable disclosures. Lisa Servon has been writing excellent columns on how for many un- and underbanked people in the United States, such services are attractive because they provide trust and intimacy through personal relationships; she has also been pointing out the diminishing gap in terms of fees and nontransparent disclosures between banks and nonbank service providers like check-cashing outlets; see "The High Cost, for the Poor, of Using a Bank," *The New Yorker*, October 9, 2013; available online at http://www.newyorker.com/currency-tag/the-high-cost-for-the-poor-of-using-a-bank#entry-more.

4. The Evolution of Money

The classic statement of money solving the "double coincidence of wants" is William Stanley Jevons, *Money and the Mechanism of Exchange* (New York: D. Appleton & Co., 1875).

A wonderful and sustained critique, which also maps out the history of money from the beginning of time to the present, is David Graeber's magnificent though controversial *Debt: The First 5,000 Years* (Hoboken, NJ: Melville House, 2011).

For my own take on the controversy, see "David Graeber's Wunderkammer, 'Debt: The First 5,000 Years,'" *Anthropological Forum* 23(1): 79–93, 2013.

5. Use Cases for Money

Georg Simmel's *Philosophy of Money* (originally published 1907; London: Routledge, 2004) should be read together with Viviana Zelizer and Jane Guyer (cited in the further reading section of chapter 2).

Many of the examples discussed in this chapter would be considered cases of earmarking or sequestering state-issued money to mark social relationships or create new ones. The classic work on this is Viviana Zelizer, *The Social Meaning of Money* (New York: Basic Books, 1995). Readers may also find my review essay "The Anthropology of Money" of interest, *Annual Review of Anthropology* 35(1): 15–36, 2006.

Many of the examples provided in this chapter came from students in my class on the anthropology of money between 2004 and 2009, and I owe them a debt of gratitude for their excellent work. Some of the examples come from the Institute for Money, Technology and Financial Inclusion; readers may wish to explore this blog at http://blog.imtfi.uci.edu.

Finally, go out and start noticing all the things people do with money objects and technologies! Make some money origami or create some art on a digital signature pad, like the artist Troy Kreiner and his colleagues; see http://troykreiner.com/john-hancock.

6. What's in Your Wallet?

The image of the contents of my own wallet unintentionally evokes the trompe l'oeil money paintings of late nineteenth- and early twentieth-century American art (with a few contemporary exponents, like the living artist Gayle B. Tate). Interested readers should consult *Old Money: American Trompe L'Oeil Images of Currency* (New York: Berry Hill Galleries, 1988).

The privatization of national currencies is an old dream of the political right. See F. A. von Hayek's *Denationalization of Money: An Analysis of the Theory and Practice of Concurrent Currencies* (Albuquerque, NM: Transatlantic Arts, 1977).

On the increasing use of noncash payments, and their implications for regulatory policy, see the periodically released U.S. Federal Reserve's

Payments Study, which documents the volume of cash and noncash transactions by payment type.

For more information on alternative and complementary currencies, readers should begin with Peter North's excellent *Money and Liberation: The Micropolitics of Alternative Currency Movements* (Minneapolis, MN: University of Minnesota Press, 2007).

Heonik Kwon writes on ghost money in "The Dollarization of Vietnamese Ghost Money," *Journal of the Royal Anthropological Institute* 13(1): 73–90, 2007.

7. What Can You Do with a Mobile Phone?

There is a growing literature on the social, political, and economic implications of the mobile phone.

On cellphone activism in Africa, see SMS *Uprising: Mobile Activism in Africa*, edited by Sokari Ekine (Cape Town: Pambazuka Press, 2010). For India, see Assa Doron and Robin Jeffrey, *The Great Indian Phone Book: How the Cheap Cell Phone Changes Business, Politics, and Daily Life* (Cambridge, MA: Harvard University Press, 2013).

For a comprehensive ethnographic account of the use of the mobile phone and its relationship to economic development, see Heather Horst and Daniel Miller's *The Cell Phone: An Anthropology of Communication* (Oxford: Berg, 2006). Another series of ethnographic studies is contained in *Personal, Portable, Pedestrian: Mobile Phones in Japanese Life*, edited by Mizuko Ito, Daisuke Okabe, and Misa Matsuda (Cambridge, MA: MIT Press, 2006). Clifford Geertz's discussion of Gilbert Ryle is contained in "Thick Description: Toward an Interpretive Theory of Culture," in *The Interpretation of Cultures: Selected Essays* (New York: Basic Books, 1973), 3–30.

This chapter also relies on the following studies: Genevieve Bell, "No More SMS from Jesus: Ubicomp, Religion, and Techno-Spiritual Practices," Proceedings of Ubicomp 2006, 141–158; Jonathan Donner, "Blurring Livelihoods and Lives: The Social Uses of Mobile Phones and Socioeconomic Development," *Innovations: Technology, Governance, Globalization* 4(1), 91–101, 2009; Jonathan Donner, "The Rules of Beeping: Exchanging Messages via Intentional 'Missed Calls' on Mobile Phones," *Journal of Computer-Mediated Communication* 13(1): 1–22, 2007; Nimmi Rangaswami and Supriya Singh, "Personalizing the Shared Mobile Phone: Internationalization, Design, and Global Development," *Lecture Notes in Computer Science* 5623: 395–403, 2009; and Nithya Sambasivan, Ed Cutrell, Kentaro Toyama, and Bonnie Nardi, "Intermediated Technology Use in Developing Communities," Proceedings of the 28th International Conference on Human Factors in Computing Systems, 2010; http://portal.acm.org /citation.cfm?id=1753326.1753718.

8. Airtime

Jan Chipchase documented the use of airtime as currency on his blog, http://www.janchipchase. com, as early as 2005.

In August 2010 there were rumors of airtime being used in Papua New Guinea to purchase a car. The GSM Association has published a comprehensive report on mobile money regulation; see Simone di Castri, *Mobile Money: Enabling Regulatory Solutions* (London: GSMA, 2013).

My own work has explored the airtime/mobile money interface; see "Mobile Money: Communication, Consumption, and Change in the Payments Space," *Journal of Development Studies* 48(5): 589–604, 2012.

9. Monetary Repertoires

Jane Guyer and Viviana Zelizer have already made an appearance in earlier chapters. Annette Weiner's *Inalienable Possessions: The Paradox of Keeping While Giving* (Berkeley: University of California Press, 1992) and Parker Shipton's *Mortgaging the Ancestors: Ideologies of Attachment in Africa* (New Haven, CT: Yale University Press, 2009) are useful touchstones for thinking about the value of illiquid assets.

The late C. K. Prahalad's *Fortune at the Bottom of the Pyramid* (originally published in 2004; Boston: Pearson Education and Wharton School Publishing, 2010) has been on the lips of many mobile money researchers and developers since I began research in the area.

Stuart Rutherford's *The Poor and Their Money* has also gone into a new printing since I began this project, and is cited chapter and verse by many in the mobile money community (originally published 2001 by Oxford India; republished by Practical Action, 2010).

Daryl Collins, Jonathan Morduch, Stuart Rutherford, and Orlanda Ruthven's *Portfolios of the Poor: How the World's Poor Live on $2 a Day* (Princeton, NJ: Princeton University Press, 2009), really reopened the discussion in microfinance circles on the savings behavior of poor people in the developing world.

Index

EBT (Electronic Benefit Transfer) card, 58

ecologies, of money, 48, 130

economics, 102, 104, 132

efficiency attribute, 68–70, 69

electronic charge card networks, 9–11, 21, 23–25

ethics, and monetary repertoires, 136–137

evolution of money: about, 63–64, 76; alternative and complementary currencies and, 73, 75, 75, 81; barter system and, 28, 63–64, 68, 75, 101; debt and, 47, 76; "double coincidence of wants" and, 28, 65; efficiency and, 68–70, 69; exchange and, 65, 76; infrastructures and, 70–73, 72, 76, 78; mobile phone-based money services and, 63; money as consumer good and, 75; payment systems and, 67, 71, 76; politics and, 66, 67; precious metals and, 65, 67; shells and, 44, 65–67, 66, 100; social relationships and, 65, 67, 70; "stages" of money and, 68; state-issued currency and, 73, 75–76; trade and, 64–65; value of exchange and, 63–65, 67; (intrinsic) value of items and, 65–67, 66;

virtual environments and, 71; wealth and, 70–71

exchange, money as, 7, 27–28, 65, 76. *See also* value of exchange

feature phones, basic, 9, 11, 73, 108

fees/costs. *See* costs/fees

formal versus informal economy, 20, 21, 40, 42, 46, 121, 125, 131–132, 134, 139–140

fungibility: of airtime minutes, 46, 116, 121, 125–126; of money, 46, 80, 92, 116, 126; payment systems and, 80, 92, 97, 99–100, 101

fun or playful activities, 90, 91

GCASH, 13, 130–131, 131

Geertz, Clifford, 114

ghost money, 102, 104

gifts: efficiency and, 68–70, 69; gift cards and, 30, 53, 54, 67–68, 91, 97, 138; paper gift certificates and, 97, 99; rituals and, 81–84, 82, 83, 84, 85; state-issued currency as, 81–84, 82, 83, 84, 85

global North (developed world): digital currency in, 37, 39; disruptions in money and, 3–4, 13, 21, 25, 26; mobile money

M-Pesa in Kenya: description and history of, 5, 9, 11, 18, 21, 130–131; mobile money and, 3, 25, 27; nonbank services and, 11, 19; poor people's lives and, 13, 21, 32–33; religious practices and, 136; Safaricom and, 3; SIM cards for, 72, 110; text messaging and, 18, 21

National Bank Act of 1863, 29
NFC (near field communication) chip, 71
nonbank services, 11, 19, 21, 32, 57
noncash payments: costs/fees for, 22, 132; mobile phones and, 37; regulations for, 97, 99, 101–102; state-issued currency linkage with, 100. *See also* cash and cash payments; cash economy; private currencies; *specific noncash payments*
nonstate currencies, 29, 37, 73, 97, 100–104, 101, 103; economics and, 102, 104; politics and, 102, 104; social relationships and, 102, 104. *See also* barter system
North, global (developed world). *See* global North (developed world)

online shopping, 27, 53

paychecks, digital transactions, 40, 55
payment systems: change and, 7; costs/fees and, 21–22; credit cards and, 23, 37, 39; ecologies of money and, 130; evolution of money and, 67, 71, 76; fungibility and, 80, 92, 97, 99–100, 101; future of, 4–5, 13, 37, 81, 143; in global North, 44; hacked systems and, 22–25, 27; infrastructures and, 18, 28, 31, 33, 39, 41; interactions within, 7, 30; iPhone, 3–4, 18, 24, 63, 142; mobile money and, 3–4; mobile phones and, 46; money and, 27–33, 31; money as redesigned/reimagined and, 4–5, 141, 143; peer-to-peer, 3–4, 30, 37, 38, 75; research on, 3, 7, 9, 46, 80, 113, 125, 132, 134–135. *See also* cash and cash payments; disruptions in money; *specific payment systems*
PayPal, 9, 63
PayPass, 24
peer-to-peer payments, 3–4, 30, 37, 38, 75
physical assets, of poor people, 44, 59, 100, 134–135, 137
point-of-sale (POS) terminals, 24, 39, 41, 58, 68, 71
politics: monetary repertoires